CIHM
Microfiche
Series
(Monographs)

ICMH
Collection de
microfiches
(monographies)

Institute for Historical Microreproductions / Institut canadien de microreproductions histo

best quality
and legibility
with the

Les images suivantes ont été reproduites avec le plus grand soin, compte tenu de la condition et de la netteté de l'exemplaire filmé, et en conformité avec les conditions du contrat de filmage.

...vers are filmed
ending on
...trated impres-
...opriate. All
...inning on the
...ed impres-
...ith a printed

Les exemplaires originaux dont la couverture en papier est imprimée sont filmés en commençant par le premier plat et en terminant soit par la dernière page qui comporte une empreinte d'impression ou d'illustration, soit par le second plat, selon le cas. Tous les autres exemplaires originaux sont filmés en commençant par la première page qui comporte une empreinte d'impression ou d'illustration et en terminant par la dernière page qui comporte une telle empreinte.

...icrofiche
...ing "CON-
...ng "END"),

Un des symboles suivants apparaîtra sur la dernière image de chaque microfiche, selon le cas: le symbole ➔ signifie "A SUIVRE", le symbole ▼ signifie "FIN".

...ilmed at
...o large to be
...e filmed
...rner, left to
...ames as
...ustrate the

Les cartes, planches, tableaux, etc., peuvent être filmés à des taux de réduction différents. Lorsque le document est trop grand pour être reproduit en un seul cliché, il est filmé à partir de l'angle supérieur gauche, de gauche à droite, et de haut en bas, en prenant le nombre d'images nécessaire. Les diagrammes suivants illustrent la méthode.

3

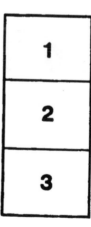

MICROCOPY RESOLUTION TEST CHART

(ANSI and ISO TEST CHART No 2)

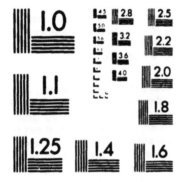

APPLIED IMAGE Inc

1653 East Main Street
Rochester, New York   14609   A
(716) 482 - 0300 - Phone
(716) 288 - 5989 - Fax

THE

Influence of the English People

UPON

Constitutional Government

FRANK B. KELLOGG, Esq.

St. Paul, Minnesota

A Canadian Bar Association

W. J. McWHINNEY, K.C.

Toronto, Ontario

Addresses delivered at the Annual Meeting

of the

...TOBA BAR ASSOCIATION

at Winnipeg, January 24th, 1914

KF Kellogg, F.
4485 The influence of the English
K42 people upon constitutional govern
ment. 1914.

THE

Influence of the English People

UPON

Constitutional Government

FRANK B. KELLOGG, Esq.

St. Paul, Minnesota

A Canadian Bar Association

W. J. McWHINNEY, K.C.

Toronto, Ontario

Addresses delivered at the Annual Meeting

of the

MANITOBA BAR ASSOCIATION

held at Winnipeg, January 24th, 1914

The Influence of the English People upon Constitutional Government.

FRANK B. KELLOGG, ESQ., ST. PAUL, MINN.

The two great civilizations of the world have been the Roman and the Anglo-Saxon. I use the term "Anglo-Saxon" instead of "English" because it is more comprehensive.

It is true that representative government was first established in England, and it has spread over most of the civilized world by the influence of the English speaking peoples. But the principles underlying representative government have a Teutonic origin, far back of English history, after Rome had ceased to be a republic and had spread its dominion over all of Western Europe.

We find, therefore, two distinct ideas of government, the Roman and the English; each in its place a great instrument of civilization in the advancement of learning and science of government and in the inculcation of the principles of Christianity.

But the theory of government of the Roman Empire was the opposite of the Anglo-Saxon. It knew nothing of representative assemblies; its popular assemblies were those simply of Rome and were primary meetings. In the zenith of power it was either a republican oligarchy or an aristocracy; in its later days a military despotism. All power flowed from the central government to its governing agencies in its conquered provinces; it received from these colonies none of the vital forces so necessary to the stability and endurance of government. This may have been a necessity in order to maintain its supremacy over alien peoples unfitted for the exercise of self-government; but, nevertheless, it was not a government which inspired its governed people with aspirations and hopes of advancement. The old phrase, "to be a Roman was to be a king" did not apply to the citizens of Britain, Gaul, Germany, or its Asiatic provinces. It was unquestionably the greatest civilizing agency of ancient times. Its laws were wise and benevolent. It spread commerce, learning, arts and sciences over the Western world. It dispelled the darkness of paganism and

3

idolatry and established in their places, Christianity. **The** causes which made it possible to extend its power and dominion over nearly all the then civilized world, largely resulted in its decay and decline. The people of its conquered provinces had no part in its government. It was inevitable that in world growth it was to pass away, and there must arise upon its ruins other and more advanced civilizations. Notwithstanding the fact that the Roman Empire began to disintegrate in the Fifth Century, it gave to nearly all of Western Europe its laws, customs and literature. Self-government was practically unknown except in England at the close of the Sixteenth Century. Complete dominance by monarchial and military power never existed among the English speaking peoples. The Anglo-Saxon civilization always was permeated by a strong, intense individualism. These characteristics had their origin far back among the tribes of Central Germany, from which England took its name. The Moot (meet), or meeting of the village, was the origin of England's local self-government, and which, with the town meeting of the United States, have been mighty factors of education and independence. It was this strong sense of individual liberty, this participation in the village meeting and in the affairs of government, which, transplanted by the Saxon, developed in England that love of self-government and respect for public opinion which made her the "Mother of Parliaments."

It is true that after the settlement of England by the Saxons, these principles of government came near to eradication through the Norman Conquest and the aggressions of the Crown, aided by the influence of Rome; but they were too deeply imbedded in the very life of the people to be entirely destroyed.

On the other hand, the influence of Rome had a salutary effect upon England. The study of her laws and literature added greatly to the culture and learning of her people and the betterment of her system of government. But the English ideas of government were totally opposite to those of the Romans, and represented principles of profound significance in the development of government which were foreign to that other great civilization.

The English idea of self-government was through representative assemblages. These assemblages, local and national, were great educators and civilizers. They inculcated principles of individual independence and stability of character, the necessary foundation of a great influential people.

It was not until the Thirteenth Century, however, that the principles upon which constitutional government rests

were clearly defined and expressed in the form of constitutional guaranties. Seven hundred years ago the Fifteenth of June, 1915, occurred at Runnymede, an event of surpassing importance in the growth of world civilization. There were laid the foundations of individual security and constitutional government. Seven centuries have come and gone since were written those memorable words wh ch constitute the basic principles of personal liberty. In those centuries the Anglo-Saxon race has carried these principles to every civilized country. They have been fixed by written constitutions and sanctified by the blood of this race. We are to-day, in your country and mine, living beneath the protection of those guaranties and working out the great destiny of self-government.

Lord Chatham once said that Magna Charta, the Petition of Right and the Bill of Rights constitute the "Bible of the English Constitution." These documents of 1215, 1628 and 1689, did not pretend to be annunciations of new principles, but rather the declaration of inalienable rights of Englishmen in their relation to society, of which they had been deprived by the usurpation of the Crown. They were the result of gradual growth and experience of a race of people strongly imbued with principles of individual liberty and self-government. It is unnecessary for me, speaking to English lawyers, to dwell upon the importance of these declarations. Amplified by experience and applied to the varied conditions of the English speaking people the world over, they constitute the groundwork of modern constitutional government. Though for centuries the guaranties of Magna Charta were violated by the Crown, and it remained for later generations to give them complete force and to realize the fruition of their promises, yet they were never lost sight of in the government of England.

The participation of the citizen in self-government—the exercise of the prerogative of citizenship—is a great aid in the development of human character. To it is largely due the growth of the Anglo-Saxon race and the supremacy of constitutional government in the world. Let us see to what extent this system has been adopted. Constitutional representative government includes, of course, constitutional monarchies; constitutional democracies; I mean unwritten as well as written constitutions. The close of the Eighteenth and beginning of the Nineteenth Century, was a great period in world history. It was the beginning of the disappearance of absolute monarchies and the establishment of constitutional monarchies and republics. During this period there appeared upon the stage great thinkers and students of government. Montesquieu, Turgot, Voltaire and Rosseau had been students of the

English system and had given to the world their masterly dissertations upon the principles underlying representative government, which contributed very largely to shape the course of the French Revolution. This revolution, unlike the evolutionary process which had been at work in England for centuries, swept away in one great upheaval the entire structure of monarchial government, and undertook to substitute the enlightened principles taught by Rosseau and Montesquieu.

That France failed for nearly a century to realize the fruition of her hopes, was due to no error in the principles of democracy or constitutional representative government, but to the fact that such a government is the product of evolution rather than revolution. At the very time when Burke was thundering his anathemas against the excesses and defects of the French republic, we doubt if he realized that England was laying the foundations of one of the greatest representative democracies of the world. It was, I believe, at this very time that parliament passed the bill for the division of the Province of Canada and the establishment of a separate legislature for each division. But he was right when with almost prophetic vision he said of the French people: "They little know how many a weary step is to be taken before they can form themselves into a mass which has a true political personality."

Written constitutions containing bills of rights first made their appearance among the American colonies in the seventeenth century. I think the first written constitution or voluntary compact of government was adopted by the colony of Connecticut in 1639, of which the charter of 1662 and the constitution of 1818 were necessary outgrowths. This constitution vested the supreme power of the commonwealth in a general court to be composed of the governor, magistrates and deputies from the several towns. It provided for an annual election by a majority vote of the whole body of freemen by ballot; that two general assemblies or courts must be held yearly. The power to make and repeal laws, to levy taxes, to admit freemen and to dispose of unappropriated lands was exclusively in the general court. One remarkable statement in this earliest constitution should not be overlooked. The only allegience it exacted was "to the government of the jurisdiction of Connecticut," the only "supreme authority" it recognized was that of the body of freemen and the general courts which they represented by their deputies. It demanded obedience to no laws except such as "are or shall be made by the lawful authority here established and for want thereof the rule of the word of God."

This constitution was written by Thomas Hooker, a distinguished preacher, and was adopted by Englishmen

who drew their inspiration from English institutions. The constitution of Maryland was adopted in 1776, and Massachusetts in 1780.

These constitutions, very naturally, were modeled after the declarations of Magna Charta, the Petition and Bill of Rights, and contained declarations of rights very similar to those adopted in the Constitution of the United States shortly after. But it is not my intention to discuss in detail the various constitutions—rather to treat of their principles in the aggregate. These constitutions, in the main, did not annunciate new principles, but such as had been asserted, tried and become fixed and established by the successive generations of our race.

The three great significant and controlling principles of these constitutions were: representative government; the division of that government into the legislative, the executive and the judicial branches, each to be independent of the others; and the declaration of rights. These constitutions have a great similarity whether adopted in constitutional monarchies or republics. It is unnecessary for me to discuss at any great length the real principles which lay at the foundation of this form of government. The legislative branch was the distinctive feature of representative government, whereby the people were directly to express their wishes; with elections frequent enough to insure proper response to public demand, without submitting the government to the instability arising from constant changes in public sentiment caused by waves of passion and popular prejudice which at times agitate all peoples and find their easiest expression in unrestrained, pure democracies.

The principle of representation is necessary in the government of countries containing great populations and wide extent of territory, for direct exercise of all governmental functions by the people is there impossible. The primary system is only practical in small communities, or in the election of individuals where the whole people may express their choice. It is, of course, impractical for general legislation, except as a restrictive force upon legislative bodies.

Under these constitutions, each branch of the government is made independent and not subject to the power of the others. It is necessary that the legislative branch shall not be subject to the influence of the executive; that the executive branch shall be represented by a single person—a hereditary monarch or an elective officer—that there shall be responsibility to a single head in order to insure prompt and intelligent execution of the law; and, lastly, and most important of all, that the judicial branch, charged with the

7

high duty of construing the constitution and laws and enforcing the rights of the people, shall be independent of the other two branches. This latter provision in the Constitution of the United States was the greatest contribution to government made by our Constitutional Convention. The English Judiciary has been independent since the Settlement Act of 1701; but England not having a written constitution, the guaranties of liberty which had been established by Magna Charta, the Petition and Bill of Rights and other Acts of Parliament, were largely dependent for their maintenance upon the legislative branch of the government. Under a written constitution these guaranties are not dependent upon the legislative branch of the government, but are protected by the judiciary; and the courts are, therefore, charged with the important duty of deciding whether the legislative or executive branches have exceeded their authority under the constitution. This form of constitutional government, while new, was not purely an experiment. It had to a large extent been in existence in the states and colonies preceding the Constitution of the United States. Nevertheless, this power has not been exercised in the United States without criticism, and it has given rise to an agitation against the courts which I believe to be not only unwise, but unjustifiable. It has created two schools of thought—those who believe in unlimited power of legislative assemblies, and those who believe in constitutional restrictions upon the exercise of this governmental function.

The advocates of pure democracy say there should be no limitations upon the legislative power—that the people are capable of governing themselves and have a right to pass any law they please, and that there should be no vested rights in individuals which the majority of the people, through legislative assemblies, may not take away. The advocates of this school point to the English Constitution as the chief source of their authority. It is undoubtedly true that in England the people depend principally upon Parliament for the maintenance of these principles of personal liberty and property rights, but England is the country where these constitutional principles had their origin and growth. There they have become imbedded in the very structure of government and fortified by long usage and tradition. And yet, even in England the parliament has, in some of its modern legislation, exercised a power over private rights which a few years ago would have been considered revolutionary and which has stirred deep opposition. I am not prepared to say that these laws are unwise; in fact, I believe most of them to be wise and that they are great steps forward in solving some of the most difficult problems of the modern social order. But, on

the other hand, it must be admitted that in my country, our system of government, our habits, customs, thoughts and traditions are along the line of written constitutional government containing restrictions upon legislative and executive power. No one will dispute the capacity of the people for self-government; but government is something more than the constant trial of experiments; there are some principles which it will do well not to depart from. The framers of the American Constitution believed in the principles of democracy; but they believed, as ages of experience had taught, that men are abusive of power; that pure democracies have never permanently existed without developing those abuses in the worst form; that a government consisting of a single power, whether it be the legislature of the pure democracy or the ruler of an empire in an absolute monarchy, is subject to the greatest abuses; that there are certain principles of government necessary to personal liberty, the security of property and the stability and permanency of institutions.

When the Federal Constitution came before the various states for ratification, there arose a general public demand for its amendment because of the omission of these very guarantees insured to Englishmen by Magna Charta and the Bill of Rights; and had it not been for the fact that there was a general sentiment created in favor of the amendment of the Constitution immediately after its adoption, it is probable that it never would have been adopted by all of the States taking part in the Constitutional Convention. This gave rise to the adoption of the first ten amendments ratified on the fifteenth of December, 1791, commonly known as the Bill of Rights.

The advocates of unlimited legislative power should occasionally pause and read the principles of the Bill of Rights, consider their source, the struggles of Englishmen for their adoption, the sacrifices to perpetuate them, and contemplate whether they would be willing to expunge any of them from our Constitution. We have been so long secure in our persons, property and homes, in the right of free speech, assemblage and petition, in the right to trial by jury, in the guaranty that no man should be twice put in jeopardy nor compelled to be a witness against himself, nor be deprived of his life, liberty or property without due process of law, that we have almost forgotten the importance of these immortal declarations and the struggles of the centuries to establish them.

It is perfectly evident that where a written constitution places restrictions upon legislative and executive power, in order to enforce them there must be an independent judiciary to declare such acts invalid. It has been said that we are the only country where such power is

vested in the judiciary. This is not correct. I sat in the gallery of the House of Lords during the last winter and heard the judgment of the Privy Council declare a law of one of the provinces of Canada invalid because transcending the limitations of the British North America Act, which is known as the Constitution of this great Dominion.

Webster, in his great speech on the independence of the judiciary, said:

"The Constitution being the supreme law, it follows, of course, that every act of the legislature contrary to that law must be void. But who shall decide this question? Shall the legislature itself decide it? If so, then the Constitution ceases to be legal and becomes only a moral restraint on the legislature. If they and they only are to judge whether their acts are to be conformable to the Constitution, then the Constitution is admonitory or advisory only—not legally binding, because if the construction of it rests wholly with them their discretion in particular cases may be in favor of very erroneous and dangerous construction. Hence, the courts of law, necessarily, when the case arises, must decide upon the validity of a particular act."

To the advocates of unlimited democracy we may point to the fact that the Constitution has stood the test of time for more than a century and a quarter. It has met the approbation and high encomiums of the statesmen of this period. Gladstone said it was one of the greatest works ever conceived and written by the pen of man. It has been found adequate to govern the people when as a nation we were but a few states along the Atlantic Coast, and to govern the nation extending from ocean to ocean, expanded in wealth, industry and progress beyond the dreams of its founders.

It may be interesting for a moment to see the extent to which the Anglo-Saxon idea of representative government has been adopted in the world. The principles of representative constitutional government have been adopted by nearly all civilized peoples and to-day is the ruling principle of the world. Constitutions similar to the British and American Constitutions have been adopted by many countries. Among these are the various constitutions of the French Republic—the last adopted February 25, 1875, following the Franco-Prussian war; the Swiss Confederation, adopted May 29, 1874; the Argentine Republic in 1853, modified in 1860 and again in 1898; Brazil in 1891; Chili in 1833; Costa Rica in 1871; Santa Domingo in 1844, modified in 1865 and 1896; Mexico in 1857. Also Bolivia and Columbia, the exact dates of which I am unable to state. In addition to these, the Dominion of Canada adopted a constitution granted to it by Great Britain in

1867; the North German Confederation in 1866; the German Empire in 1871; the Netherlands in 1815, revised in 1844, 1848 and 1887. England granted a written constitution to Australia in 1890, and afterwards to its colonies in South Africa. Written constitutions have been adopted in Spain, Italy, Norway, Sweden, Belgium and Austria-Hungary.

It is impossible for me in the time at my disposal to compare these various constitutions and show the similarity of their provisions with those of the English and American constitutions. It is sufficient to say that the principles established are the same. It was largely through the influence of the Anglo-Saxon race that the other countries of Europe and of the western hemisphere have adopted principles of representative government. The influence of these institutions in the education and advancement of the people is difficult to measure. It has been far-reaching and potent. It has been to a large extent the cause of the wonderful advancement in education, intellectual and material conditions during the last century. For government is inseparably bound up with the prosperity, happiness and progress of the people. Their moral, intellectual and physical development is dependent very largely upon these benevolent principles.

It is remarkable to see to what extent Bills of Rights have been established by written constitutions. They will be found in the constitutions of the Republic of Argentine, Chili, Brazil, Switzerland, Mexico, and also in the Netherlands, Norway, Denmark, Japan, Portugal, Spain, Sweden and Belgium. With the exception of Magna Charta and the Bill of Rights of the English Constitution, written guaranties of rights were practically unknown to governments prior to the eighteenth century. It was the absence of these guaranties and the fact that the maintenance of these rights were dependent upon the caprice of those in authority, rather than upon settled rules of law, that led to the adoption of written constitutions and the establishment of independent judiciaries to enforce them.

Taking up these various constitutions and noting the similarity in their provisions, we first come to the executive. In all the republics, provision is made for the election of a president, who is the chief executive head. This is accomplished through an electoral college, or the election by the Senate and House of Representatives or the body corresponding thereto, or by a direct vote of the people. The powers of the executives may vary somewhat, but there is a great uniformity, and there are many limitations upon these powers in the Constitutions. There is remarkable uniformity in the legislative departments of these various governments. I believe without exception they are divided into two chambers corresponding to our House of Repre-

11

sentatives and Senate or to the British or Canadian Parliaments.

In many instances, the names, the manner of election and the powers are substantially the same, the representatives being the most popular body, elected at short intervals, therefore being more directly expressive of the will of the people.

With one exception none of the Constitutions provide for the initiative and referendum as the ordinary means of legislation. True, there is limited referendum in the amendment of constitutions. In Switzerland in 1906 the council presented to the Federal Assembly of the Republic of Switzerland a project for the revision of the constitution extending popular initiative to Federal legislation. The project was debated in the National Council in December, 1906; was referred back to the Federal Council for further report, and subsequently was adopted, whereby steps towards legislative action may be taken by means of the popular initiative and laws passed by the Federal Assembly may be vetoed by the popular voice. Whenever a petition demanding the revision or annulment of a measure passed by the legislature is presented by 30,000 citizens, or the alteration is demanded by eight cantons, the law in question must be submitted to the direct vote of the nation. But the Assembly remains the principal legislative body of the Confederation of Switzerland. Except as a corrective, to a very limited extent, the initiative and referendum nowhere prevails as a means of legislation among the republics or empires of the civilized world.

In all the republics and constitutional monarchies thus established since the adoption of our Constitution, the independency of the judiciary has been deemed of the most vital importance.

In nearly all, the judges are appointed and the tenure of office is for life, or during good behavior. There is no such thing as the recall of judges in any of them, except in a few of the states of the United States. In Italy, the judges may be removed during the first three years of their term. This indicates a world-wide appreciation of the fact that the judicial office is different from that of the executive or legislative, and that its independence is of the most vital importance to the stability of the government, the maintenance of liberty and the preservation of law.

I have thus imperfectly sketched the work of the Anglo-Saxon race in world civilization. In this work the lawyer has borne a great and honorable part. In the field of literature he has filled the highest position and met the greatest responsibilities. We cannot forget in those formative years of English institutions the heroic stand of many great

lawyers for the rights and liberties of the people against arbitrary power. His work has been woven into the fabric of constitutions and laws of the English speaking nations. His influence was never more potent, or services in greater need, than at the present time. We are not confronted with the dangers which surrounded the men who developed this Anglo-Saxon civilization, but we are confronted with other problems of equal magnitude. The tremendous increase and concentration of wealth, with its consequent power, the great development in invention and science applied to industry, the increase in rapid transportation and the concentration of population in the cities, have raised problems of government control and of social development which require the greatest constructive ability of modern statesmenship. These things are the result of the marvelous development of the human race under the most favorable conditions.

During the last ten year. in the United States we have been trying to work out the problems growing out of the concentration of wealth. The abuse of power of these great aggregations of capital commonly known as "trusts," was responsible for the agitation. This abuse of power has been almost entirely stopped, and I believe to-day that business is being conducted upon a higher plane morally and ethically than ever before in our history; that business men are doing more for their employees on material, physical and educational lines than ever before; that they are more mindful of the public interest and that large enterprises are being conducted to-day in conformity with the law. This has been accomplished by the same processes of self-government which have been distinctive characteristics of the Anglo-Saxon race for centuries. When it is necessary to reform government they have grappled the problems with the grim determination to accomplish it. When it is necessary to reform business methods, they have done it in the same way. That mistakes have been made, excesses committed and some injury done to public and private interests in this process of reform is undoubted, but it has always been the case with the march of progress. It is the province of the lawyer more than any other citizen to lead these reforms along legal and constitutional steps. He can thus be a progressive force in society, at the same time conserving the best interests of the people. The lawyer who places the welfare of his country above personal gain and aids in solving these problems will meet the highest ideals of his profession.

A Canadian Bar Association.

W. J. McWHINNEY, K.C., TORONTO, ONT.

Mr. President and Gentlemen of the Manitoba Bar Association:—

I am asked to speak to you on the formation of a Canadian Bar Association—a question by no means free of difficulties and requiring very careful thought and consideration. Some few years ago the subject was mooted and discussed at some length by the Ontario Bar Association and its Council resolved to feel the pulse of the Associations of the Sister Provinces and to our communications two replies were received. Need I say we were very much discouraged. Since then the present Minister of Justice addressed you in favour of such an organization and has since spoken at our last Banquet in most cheerful and encouraging words so that we know we have his hearty approval and will receive his valued co-operation. In justice to him—Sir—as well as to ourselves we must see that we proceed cautiously and build on a workable foundation so that the structure may not only be reared but on such a basis and with aims and objects which when developed will result for the general good of all and justify its existence. Experience has taught us—Sir—that it is easy to organize and from thence the way is difficult and those who should be members and energetic supporters are deeply engrossed with their own interests and accumulations and indifferent to the interest of the Profession in general. I assure you our task in Ontario, where we have 1,746 members of the Profession including 5 women, one-third of whom live in Toronto and about one-third members of our Association, has been arduous and at times dispiriting mainly because we could not justify, in the opinion of the many, that our efforts as an Association had been fruitful of results. The merely fraternal and social side proved insufficient in itself, therefore by our fruits they demanded we must be known and our past two years have been more strenuously devoted to fruit bearing and in addition to suggesting and influencing reforms in legisatlion we have produced a consolidation of our Rules of Practice from about 1,400 to 700 odd, a block system of tariff of costs, new Surrogate Court Rules

and Forms and a more congenia! tariff in Surrogate matters. These preliminaries to forewarn you that the task your subject deals with is not a light one or rashly to be undertaken.

You have been advised of our Association's resolution in favour of your suggestion to form such an Association and the Committee appointed to deal with it has met and gravely discussed it and our Council has authorized me to convey to you the views of the Committee so far as developed as they have not yet been so matured as to report to Council. Obstacles many have been considered and the chief ones I have alluded to very briefly. I am pleased, however, to be able to say our Committee views the Association as a possibility and as a reality provided certain main features can be successfully attained. These essentials are (a) The active co-operation and financial support of the Department of Justice of each Province (b) A representative on the Council from each of such Departments (c) The hearty co-operation of the Bar Association of each Province, and where none exists, the creation of a Provincial or Territorial Council to elect representatives and furnish the needful. As in truth if formed, the Association must be a working body just as much as any Board of Trade, Manufacturers Association or other trade organization and as thoroughly organized and fully equipped. It must represent the Profession as a whole and have behind it the good will and support of the Profession in general. It must have objects and work to do outside the sphere of the Benchers and similar societies at present existing in each Province and these must be such as to be of general and actual value to the Canadian community as a component part of the Great Empire. Like the American Bar Association which from small beginnings and earnest strivings, compassing now the many States of the Union as a mighty legislative organization, it must have a Kellogg and a Waddams and Mr. Kellogg will bear me out in saying such a genius as Waddams is rare and indispensable. We have the advantage of having before us the constitution of the American Bar Association and we have the goodwill of that Association and its Officers which will afford us relief in meeting many obstacles and solving difficulties without learning how by experience. From its constitution permit me to read.

(Article 1—Its object shall be to advance the science of jurisprudence, promote the administration of justice and uniformity of legislation throughout the union, uphold the honor of the profession of the law and encourage cordial intercourse among the members of the American Bar.)

the task should prepare a Constitution, fix the Provincial contribution so that each Provincial Association (and where none a local Council created for the same purpose) adopting the principle of formation should at the same time approve of three important factors:

(a) The proposed Constitution.

(b) The proposed Annual Contribution to the Association.

(c) That all members in it then qualified and in good standing should be enrolled members of the Association without further fee.

2. The formation of the first Council of the Association composed of the Honorary President, President and Secretary of each existing Provincial organization or Council created by the local members of the Profession for the purpose and the past Presidents of each Provincial Organization to be ex officio members of such first Council.

3. The Council so formed to elect its own Officers and Committees except Honorary Presidents and Vice-Presidents—and to adopt the proposed constitution approved by the Provincial organizations and Councils as the Constitution of the Association and thereafter the formation of Council and election of Officers and appointment of Committees to be in accordance with the provisions of the constitution.

4. The Honorary President to be the Hon. the Minister of Justice for the time being.

5. The Honorary Vice-Presidents to be the Attorney General of each Province and the Commissioner or other Head Official representative of the administration of Justice of each Territory.

6. The Council so formed should promptly adopt suitable By-laws as the By-laws of the Association until rescinded by the Association, should appoint a permanent secretary and treasurer and fix the place of head office.

7. The Council so formed should be promptly furnished by the Provincial Organizations and Territorial Council with certified lists of all members so becoming members of the Association, and with information as to proposed legislation in the various Provinces, and of all such subjects as should be brought before the Association at its first meeting and the Council should fix the place of the first meeting at Ottawa during the Session of Parliament and the Sittings of the Supreme Court for the convenience of members and to ensure a good attendance at the first Annual Meeting.

8. In order to effectuate two of the main features of such a body "the adoption of model acts in and the uni-

formity of the laws of the various Provinces" it is deemed essential that the Ministers of Justice and the Attorney General or other Chief Representative of the Administration of Justice in each Province and Territory should concur in the formation of the Association and should appoint a representative from his Department as a member of the Council and make a contribution to the funds of the Association as one of the expense items of his department.

The subject with us being a comparatively new one and the opportunity of studying the operations of other similar bodies since our Annual Meeting on 29th December last, having been limited, our Committee has not dealt exhaustively with the subject and only general discussions such as I have outlined have been considered of the subject matter referred to the Committee, but it is clear many desirable and commendable undertakings are open to such an Association and Canada has reached a stage when the duties of Cabinet Ministers have become very onerous and legislation of general import cannot receive well weighed consideration which is imperative to secure well framed laws—hence so many amendments, revisions, consolidations and reconsolidations, which make the labours of the Profession arduous indeed.

By way of general discussion:—There are the Insurance Laws, Policy Contracts and Statutory Conditions. Why not the same uniform Insurance Acts and conditions? A subject with which every layman should be familiar and upon which there should be no distinction ·t a uniform statute law in the Dominion as well as ... ch Province, and one standard form of policy for each ranch or distinct class of insurance; the object being to insure in effect as well as in name and not by variations in contract or conditions to defeat the very object of the legislation and why should not Insurance Companies when they part with possession of a Policy, collect the premiums as any other creditor who parts with his goods. Possession of the Policy when obtained without fraud, should be sufficient in all classes of Insurance as much as in the case of fire policies.

Uniformity of all commercial laws having especial regard to the rules of evidence and the necessity for a written contract in commercial matters. The provisions of the Quebec Civil Code on this point are very similar to those of the English Statute of Frauds. There are slight differences in the provisions of all the Provinces with regard to contracts for the sale of goods and other written contracts affecting commercial matters which should be the same in all Provinces.

The laws with respect to preferences should be the same in each Province pending the enactment, which we hope to accomplish, of a uniform bankruptcy law.

17

The Statutes with respect to conditional sales and the Factors Acts should be the same in each Province. The Statutes of Limitation should be the same in the various Provinces in so far as the same affect commercial matters. Mechanics Lien laws should be uniform in each Province. There should be one uniform Company law throughout the Provinces of Canada. The importance of uniform regulations to the financial community respecting Municipal debentures, cannot be over estimated.

With regard to the law of real property, the West is, speaking generally, ahead of the East, but there are many differences between the laws of Manitoba, Saskatchewan, Alberta and British Columbia, most of the differences being without any logical foundation. It would be advisable, if possible, to have the laws of all the Provinces, excepting perhaps Quebec, uniform in all matters relating to real property. The law of Landlord and tenant comes under this head and there is no reason why these laws should not be uniform. The law relating to Married Women might also be made uniform.

There should be one uniform law of negligence including damages for accidents resulting in death, and one uniform law for the compensation of workmen.

Uniformity of laws in respect to Judgments of the Courts of other Provinces. Canada can never hope to be a complete Nationality until the Courts of each Province are made auxiliary one to another. In the United States, they have a system of Federal Courts and State Courts. There seems to be no reason why we cannot work out all questions of jurisdiction and procedure with the existing Provincial Courts provided we adopt in some way the present example furnished by the Dominion Winding-up Act which makes a definite provision that in winding-up matters the Courts of each Province are auxiliary one to another and an Order made in one Province may be enforced as a Judgment of the Court of another Province. The present Exchequer Court has jurisdiction over the whole of Canada but only in a very limited class of matters such as Infringements of Patents. Trade Marks and Copyrights, Dominion Railways, etc. This principle might be extended so that when an action is brought in Winnipeg with the witnesses resident in Ontario the evidence might be taken or the case even tried in Ontario by a simple Order of the Winnipeg Courts. Nothing brings the administration of Justice more into disrepute than the tantalizing questions of jurisdiction and procedure, all tending to create not only unnecessary expense but delay and subsequent denial of justice. In the administration of justice in Canada it ought to be thoroughly settled that once a case is tried out in any Province, the Judgment in such Province is good and can be enforced

by every other Province without commencing proceedings de novo.

All these things are capable of accomplishment with our present legislative machinery. It needs a few trained lawyers acting under the auspices and with the approval of the Governments of the various Provinces to put these matters in order and to devise these uniform laws. This can be accomplished better through the medium of Committees of the Canadian Bar Association than in any other way. Members of the Profession with the necessary ability and knowledge for framing these laws are in the first place, too busy to pay attention to the subject, and in the second place, they would, as matters now stand, have only their trouble for their pains. If a Bar Association were once formed with sufficient funds to enable it to employ competent assistants from men who have the time and ability to do the detail work, leading members of the Profession in our Province could easily be procured who would take sufficient interest to meet members of the Profession from other Provinces and reconcile all differences, and establish general principles with regard to each point upon which differences now exist.

The lawyer of to-day and the student of to-morrow will surely play a prominent part in the present wonderful development and in the great future of this Country and a Canadian Association can be the means to this end Nothing will advance this wonderful progress more than the making of such uniform laws throughout Canada as will give confidence to the capitalist and foreign investor and may we not look forward with hope that our profession shall at least be one of the main instruments in the building up of this grand Country of ours as part of the greatest Empire the world has ever known.

Middlesbrough Football Club
An A-Z

MIDDLESBROUGH FOOTBALL CLUB AN A-Z

Dean Hayes

Aureus

First Published 2000

Cover photograph: Juninho of Middlesbrough and Gary Elkins of Wimbledon
battle it out in the 1995-96 domestic campaign. ©Brian Mackness (Prosport)

ISBN 1 899750 17 7

Printed in Great Britain.

A catalogue record for this book is available from the British Library.

Aureus Publishing Limited, 24 Mafeking Road, Cardiff, CF23 5DQ, UK.
Tel: (029) 2045 5200 Fax: (029) 2045 5200
Int. tel: +44 29 2045 5200 Int. fax: +44 29 2045 5200
E-mail: sales@aureus.co.uk
           meuryn.hughes@aureus.co.uk
Web site: www.aureus.co.uk

To Chris Sherrington wherever you may be!

Acknowledgments

I should like to express my thanks to the following organisations for their assistance:

Middlesbrough FC; The Association of Football Statisticians; The Football League Ltd; The British Newspaper Library; Middlesbrough Central library; The Harris Library.

Thanks also to the following individuals: Ben Hayes, Iain Price and George Hadfield. Thanks also to Meuryn Hughes for his continued support in the publishing of this A–Z series.

Bibliography
Let's Talk About Middlesbrough by Tom Morgan (Sentinel Publications, 1946)
Middlesbrough: A Complete Record by Harry Glasper (Breedon Books, 1989)
Middlesbrough FC The First 100 Years (Published by the club, 1976)
Middlesbrough FC by Eric Taylor (Archive Publications, 1989)
Boro's Best by Dave Allan, Adrian Bevington and Mark Hooper (Juniper Publishing, 1997)

Illustrations
Photographs have been supplied by the Lancashire Evening Post, the Bolton Chronicle and from the author's personal collection.

A

ABANDONED MATCHES

A match may be called off by the referee whilst it is in progress when conditions do not permit it to be completed.

Far fewer matches are now abandoned than were in the past. This is due to the fact that if there is some doubt about playing the full game, the match is likely to be postponed.

Billy Cook the Oldham Athletic left-back forced the referee to abandon the match against Middlesbrough on Easter Monday 1915 when he refused to leave the pitch after being sent-off.

The Latics were challenging for the First Division title but were 3–0 down after twenty minutes of the match at Ayresome Park. Early in the second-half, Cook fouled Carr and Middlesbrough's Tinsley scored from the penalty to extend their lead to 4–1. Soon after, Cook fouled Carr again and the referee had no hesitation in sending Cook off.

The Oldham players surrounded the referee to protest but he refused to change his decision and gave Cook one minute to leave the field. The referee pulled out his watch and when 60 seconds had elapsed and Cook was still on the pitch, the official walked off, abandoning the game.

The full list of abandoned games involving Middlesbrough is listed below:

Date	Opponents	Competition	Score	Reason
25.12.12	Bradford C.	Division 1	0–1	Fading Light (84min)
05.04.15*	Oldham A.	Division 1	4–1	Sending-Off (56 min)
04.02.22	Everton	Division 1	0–1	Snowstorm (57 min)
16.11.29	Arsenal	Division 1	0–1	Fog (55 min)
10.01.59	Birmingham C.	FA Cup Rd 3	1–1	Icy Pitch (60 min)
24.09.74	Leicester C.	Division 1	1–0	Floodlight Failure (29 min)

* Result stood.

AGGREGATE SCORE

Middlesbrough's highest aggregate score in any competition came in the Football League Cup competition of 1996–97. Playing Hereford United, 'Boro notched up 10 goals over the two legs. They won the first leg at the Riverside Stadium 7–0 with Ravanelli scoring four of the goals and then triumphed 3–0 at Edgar Street to win 10–0 on aggregate.

AITKEN, ANDY

Andy Aitken was one of Newcastle United's all-time great wing-halves, though he could play in a variety of roles including full-back, inside or centre-forward and in any of the midfield positions.

His first job was that of a grocer's assistant but his performances for Ayr Parkhouse led to a number of clubs showing an interest in him, notably Newton Heath and Preston North End. Aitken opted for Newcastle United and scored on his debut in a 3–0 win over Loughborough Town. Aitken went on to score 42 goals in 349 games for the Magpies, playing in every position except goalkeeper! He was appointed club captain and led the side to the League Championship and FA Cup Final in 1905 and to another final appearance twelve months later.

In October 1906 he joined Middlesbrough as player-manager and made his debut in a 1–0 home defeat by Liverpool. Aitken, who cost 'Boro £500, arrived at Ayresome Park with the club bottom of the First Division. Under his influence though they rallied to end the season in 11th place.

The following season, 1907–08, 'Boro had one of their best-ever seasons, finishing sixth in Division One, only two points behind runners-up Aston Villa. The following year, 'Boro did well again but Aitken left Ayresome Park on a sour note, following a clash of personalities with a member of the board.

His next club was Leicester Fosse but they were relegated at the end of his first season in charge. Things were worse the following season and Aitken who was still playing for Scotland at the time, returned north of the border to see out his playing career with Dundee.

ALLISON, MALCOLM

Malcolm Allison's coaching and management days have often overshadowed the fact that he was a fine centre-half in his playing days. His first club was Charlton Athletic for whom he signed in 1944 and later West Ham United. He played in 255 games for the Hammers before being struck down with tuberculosis, which resulted in him losing a lung.

Allison took up his first management post with Bath City before Plymouth Argyle gave him his first job in League football. In July 1965 he joined Joe Mercer at Manchester City to form one of the most successful partnerships in English football. One of the best coaches in the game, Allison was also one of the most explosive. In October of that year, he was suspended for a month following a series of outbursts.

Yet Mercer and Allison revived the Maine Road club. The Second Division Championship was won in 1965–66. Two years later the League title was gained and other trophies soon followed. City won the FA Cup in 1969 and the European Cup Winners' Cup and Football League Cup the following year. By 1972, Allison felt he deserved more than the tag of 'assistant' and when Mercer left for Coventry, he got his wish. After only nine months in charge, he left for Crystal Palace, saying he could no longer motivate the City players. There followed another spell at Plymouth and periods coaching in Turkey and the United States before Allison returned to Maine Road in July 1979. After a number of disastrous million pound signings, he lost his job and returned to Crystal Palace.

Later he managed Portuguese club Sporting Lisbon to a League and Cup double before being controversially sacked in the summer of 1982.

Allison then took charge at Ayresome Park but in his first season as manager, the club only managed to finish 16th in Division Two. Forced into selling some of the club's best young players and with 'Boro struggling in the lower reaches of the Second Division, he was dismissed as the gap between Allison and the Board grew wider.

Thereafter he took to travelling from one football outpost to another. Willington, County Durham and Kuwait were followed by a spell as caretaker-manager of Bristol Rovers where sadly he was dogged by ill-health.

3

Malcolm Allison

AMATEUR CUP

Inaugurated in 1893–94 when Old Carthusians became the competition's first winners, the FA Amateur Cup was won by Middlesbrough the following season. After beating Bishop Auckland, Darlington, Old Brightonians and the Lancaster Regiment (Portsmouth) in the semi-final, 'Boro met Old Carthusians in the Cup Final on 27 April 1895. A crowd of 4,000 saw 'Boro come from one goal down to win 2–1 with goals from Dave Mullen and 'Happy' Nelmes.

Middlesbrough won the trophy for a second time in 1897–98. After beating Leadgate Park, Thornaby Utopians and Casuals, 'Boro faced Thornaby in the semi-final. The tie had to be switched from Darlington following a smallpox scare and was eventually played in the isolated Cleveland hill

village of Brotton. 'Boro won the semi-final to take their place in the final at the Crystal Palace on 23 April 1898 where their opponents were Uxbridge. Goals from Bishop and Kemplay gave 'Boro the Cup.

ANDERSON, STAN

Stan Anderson captained Sunderland, Newcastle United and Middlesbrough and was capped twice by England. A tough-tackling wing-half, he played in 402 games for the Wearsiders and also appeared in two FA Cup semi-finals. He joined Newcastle United in November 1963 and played an important part in their Second Division Championship winning season of 1964–65.

In November 1965 he accepted the position of player-coach with Middlesbrough and made his debut for the Ayresome Park club against

Stan Anderson

Cardiff City, scoring one of 'Boro's goals in a 4–3 home defeat. Anderson went on to score two goals in 22 games before being appointed Middlesbrough's manager in April 1966. Unable to prevent the club from being relegated, he led 'Boro back to the Second Division in 1966–67, his first full season in charge at Ayresome Park.

After twice going close to promotion to the First Division, he left 'Boro to manage AEK Athens. He later managed Panathinaikos before returning to England to become assistant-manager of Queen's Park Rangers. In February 1975 he replaced Maurice Setters as manager of Doncaster Rovers and three years later joined Bolton Wanderers as coach. When Ian Greaves left the club, Anderson was appointed manager but was unable to prevent the Trotters from being relegated. Despite being given money to strengthen the squad, results didn't improve and in May 1981, Anderson was sacked with more than two years of his contract still to run.

ANGLO-ITALIAN CUP

When Swindon Town won the Football League Cup in 1969 they were ineligible for the Fairs Cup because they were not a First Division side. Consequently they organised a match against the Italian League Cup winners AS Roma, playing for the Anglo-Italian Cup. The following year the Anglo-Italian Cup was introduced for club sides from the two countries who had no involvement in Europe.

Middlesbrough entered the competition in 1969–70. Their results were as follows:

AS Roma	Home 1–0	Away 1–1
Lanerossi Vicenza	Home 2–0	Away 2–2

ANGLO-SCOTTISH CUP

The Anglo-Scottish Cup was inaugurated in 1975–76 following the withdrawal of Texaco from the competition of that name.

In 1975–76, 'Boro were unbeaten in the qualifying group matches, beating Sunderland (Home 3–2) and Carlisle United (Home 4–1) and drawing with Newcastle United (Away 2–2). In the first leg of the quarter-final, 'Boro beat Aberdeen 2–0 before a superb performance at Pittodrie saw the Dons beaten 5–2 to give the Ayresome Park club a 7–2 aggregate win. Mansfield Town were easily beaten in the two-legged semi-final, 3–0 at Ayresome Park and 2–0 at Field Mill as 'Boro reached

the final where their opponents were Fulham. A David Armstrong goal which was helped into the net by Fulham's Les Strong separated the teams at Ayresome Park before 'Boro played out a goalless draw at Craven Cottage, thus making them the first club to lift the Anglo-Scottish Cup.

In 1976–77, 'Boro beat Hull City (Away 2–0) and Sheffield United (Away 1–0) but were then beaten 3–0 at Newcastle United, a result which prevented them from qualifying for the knockout stages of the competition.

APPEARANCES

Tim Williamson holds the record for the highest number of League and Cup appearances for Middlesbrough with a total of 602 games to his credit between 1902 and 1923. The players with the highest number of appearances are as follows:

		League	FA Cup	FLg Cup	Others	Total
1.	Tim Williamson	563	39	-	-	602
2.	Gordon Jones	457(5)	40	26	4	527(5)
3.	John Craggs	408(1)	33	31	15	487(1)
4.	Jim Platt	401	34	33	13	481
5.	John Hickton	395(20)	37	26(4)	15(2)	473(26)
6.	George Camsell	418	35	-	-	453
7.	Jackie Carr	421	28	-	-	449
8.	David Armstrong	357(2)	29	27(1)	15	428(3)
9.	Stephen Pears	339	25	32	28	424
10.	Tony Mowbray	345(3)	23	28(2)	23(1)	419(6)

ARMSTRONG, DAVID

An England Schoolboy international, David Armstrong made his Middlesbrough debut in a 3–1 defeat at Blackpool in April 1972. After establishing himself as a first team regular towards the end of the following season, he went on to be ever-present in seven seasons, appearing in 305 consecutive league games - still a club record.

He won England Under-23 and 'B' international honours before winning his first full cap against Australia in May 1980.

He won a Second Division Championship medal in 1973–74 and towards the end of his 'Boro career was awarded a testimonial game against the Championship-winning side. Armstrong's best season in

terms of goals scored was 1979–80 when he topped the club's scoring charts with 14. He had scored 73 goals in 416 League and Cup games for 'Boro when he was transferred to Southampton in the summer of 1981 for a record £600,000.

He quickly fitted into the Saints' midfield and scored 15 goals, an impressive total in the face of some ultra-defensive football. Although naturally a left-sided player, his reading of the game allowed him to play in a variety of positions. He was an obvious choice as the club's captain and his talents earned him further international caps against West Germany and Wales while at the Dell. He had played in 262 games for the club when contractual disputes led to him leaving the Dell and joining Bournemouth where he later ended his league career. He joined Waterlooville FC as general manager in March 1995 having previously spent a number of years as an officer for Football in the Community, latterly at Reading.

David Armstrong

ASHCROFT, BILLY

Known to the Wrexham fans as 'King Billy' he made his debut for the Welsh club in a goalless draw at Reading in October 1970, just two days after his 18th birthday. He established himself in the first team midway through the 1971–72 season and ended the following campaign as the club's leading scorer. Also during that 1972–73 season he played in the club's first match in Europe against Zurich and then scored the winner in the home leg. Over the next two seasons he was hampered by injuries but in 1975–76 he returned to fitness and was again the Robins' leading scorer. Forming a good striking partnership with Graham Whittle, he scored 29 goals in 54 games during the 1976–77 season including four in a 6–0 win at Chesterfield.

After three games in the following season, Ashcroft left the Racecourse Ground to join Middlesbrough for a fee of £120,000, having scored 96 goals in 272 games for Wrexham.

Billy Ashcroft

He made his 'Boro debut in a 2–1 defeat at West Bromwich Albion, ending the campaign with six goals in 36 games as the Ayresome Park club finished 14th in Division One. He netted a similar total the following season before Middlesbrough manager John Neal switched him to centre-half with great success. He had scored 25 goals in 179 games for 'Boro before leaving to play for Dutch club Twente Enschede.

In 1985 he returned to these shores to play for Tranmere Rovers where he saw out his league career.

ASHMAN, DON
Half-back Don Ashman played part-time football for Cockfield Albion whilst working as a coal-miner. He joined Middlesbrough in the summer of 1924 for a fee of just £10 and the guarantee that 'Boro would play a friendly at Cockfield's ground.

Ashman made his debut in a 2–2 draw at Coventry in November 1924 and soon established himself as a first team regular. In 1926–27 when the club won the Second Division Championship, Ashman missed just one game and scored his first goal for the club in a 4–1 home win over Darlington. Though 'Boro were relegated after just one season in the top flight, they won promotion at the first attempt although Ashman only appeared in three games due to a series of injuries. He went on to play in 174 games before leaving to join Queen's Park Rangers in May 1932.

He was an important member of the club's Third Division (South) side but in 1935 after playing in 83 games he returned to the north-east to end his career with Darlington.

ATTENDANCE - AVERAGE
The average home league attendances of Middlesbrough over the last ten seasons have been as follows:

1990–91	17,023	1995–96	29,283
1991–92	14,703	1996–97	29,848
1992–93	16,724	1997–98	29,994
1993–94	10,400	1998–99	34,386
1994–95	18,807	1999-2000	33,393

ATTENDANCE - HIGHEST
The record attendance at Ayresome Park is 53,802 for the First Division game with Newcastle United on 27 December 1949. For the record,

'Boro won 1–0 with Peter McKennan scoring the game's only goal. The record attendance at the Riverside Stadium is 34,800 for the visit of Leeds United in a Premier League game on 26 February 2000. The game was goalless.

ATTENDANCE - LOWEST
The lowest attendance at the Riverside Stadium is 13,280 for the second round League Cup game with Rotherham United on 20 September 1995. The match ended in a 2–1 win for 'Boro with goals scored by Mustoe and Fjortoft.

AWAY MATCHES
Middlesbrough's best away win is 7–1, a scoreline achieved against Blackburn Rovers on 29 November 1947 and Derby County on 29 August 1959. The club have also scored seven goals in away matches on three other occasions - Barnsley (7–2 in 1901–02); Grimsby Town (7–4 in 1926–27) and Aston Villa (7–2 in 1935–36). Middlesbrough's worst defeat away from home is the 9–0 beating handed out by Blackburn Rovers on 6 November 1954.

AWAY SEASONS
The club's highest number of away wins came in 1986–87 when they won 12 of their 23 matches and finished runners-up to Bournemouth in the Third Division. The most away goals scored by the club is 44 in 1926–27 as 'Boro won the Second Division Championship.

AYRESOME PARK
Ayresome Park which cost just under £11,000 to build, was officially opened on 12 September 1903 when a crowd of 30,000 packed into the ground for the league match against Sunderland which the visitors won 3–2. A friendly had been played at the ground on 1 September but only 7,000 watched the game against Celtic as the ground wasn't quite ready.

In February 1905, Ayresome Park staged its first full international match when England with 'Boro's Tim Williamson in goal drew 1–1 with Ireland. The FA also chose Ayresome Park for a number of amateur international matches and in 1912 it housed its first FA Amateur Cup Final.

The first major change to the ground occurred in 1936 when the South Stand was replaced by a 9,000 capacity two-tier structure at a cost

of £13,400. Also around this time a roof was put on the West End for £2,700. Just after the Second World War, the terracing at each end of the ground was rebuilt and in December 1949, a record crowd of 53,802 attended Ayresome Park for the local derby against Newcastle United.

In 1957 floodlights were installed at a cost of £18,000 and first switched on for the visit of Sunderland in October of that year. Ayresome Park was chosen as one of the venues for the 1966 World Cup and this meant that further improvements would need to be made to the ground. A roof was put on the East End and seating installed on to the terrace whilst extra seats were put in both the North and South Stands. 'Boro at the time were a Third Division club and though 75% of the £125,000 needed to make these improvements came from FA loans and government grants, it took the club ten years to pay back its share of the cash. After the World Cup there were a number of reductions in the ground's capacity and following the Valley Parade fire, the capacity was cut from 39,500 to 10,658. On inspection it was discovered that Ayresome Park had structural defects on three sides of the ground, necessitating £100,000 to be spent on repairs and fire-proofing.

In the summer of 1986 with the club having debts of £1.8 million, liquidators were appointed and the ground's gates padlocked. Though the club were saved at the last minute, they were still barred from using Ayresome Park when the 1986–87 season got underway. Though the club eventually returned to playing its games at Ayresome Park, the ground required just under £400,000 to be spent on further repairs to achieve a capacity of 27,272. Following the Taylor Report, another £400,000 was spent on removing the perimeter fences and installing seats on the South Stand paddock. It became clear that 'Boro were not going to meet the August 1994 all-seater deadline, but they were saved from having their terraces closed by Steve Gibson who approached the Teeside Development Corporation with a view to a new ground being built in the town's dockland area.

Thus the last league game to be played at Ayresome Park was on 30 April 1995 when 'Boro beat Luton Town 2–1 in front of a 23,903 crowd to clinch the First Division Championship and a place in the Premiership.

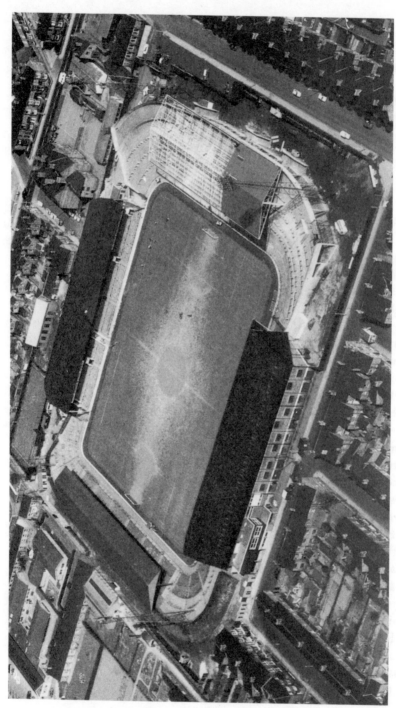

Ayresome Park

B

BAIRD, IAN

Ian Baird was an England Schoolboy international before signing professional forms for Southampton in April 1982. A strong, bustling centre-forward, he found it difficult to break into the first team on a regular basis and joined Leeds United for £50,000 in March 1985 following loan spells with Cardiff City and Newcastle United.

He was the Elland Road club's leading scorer in 1986–87 as they finished fourth in Division Two. At the end of that season he joined newly-promoted Portsmouth to play First Division football, an FA tribunal setting the fee at £285,000. Hard-up Pompey sold him back to Leeds in February 1988 for £185,000 but after Lee Chapman arrived at Elland Road, Baird, who had scored 57 goals in 192 games in his two spells, was sold to Middlesbrough in January 1990 for £500,000.

He made his 'Boro debut in a 2–0 home win over his old club, Portsmouth. Baird scored five goals in 19 games that season including two in the final match of the campaign as 'Boro beat Newcastle United 4–1 to enable the Teeside club to stay in the top flight. In 1990–91, Baird scored 14 goals including a hat-trick in a 5–2 win at Oxford United.

He left Middlesbrough to join Hearts in July 1991 for £400,000 but two years later returned to the Football League when he signed for Bristol City for £295,000. A further move took him to Plymouth Argyle in the summer of 1995, Baird later joining Brighton and Hove Albion

where he ended his league career. On leaving Albion he had a short spell as player-manager of Salisbury City before departing for Hong Kong to assist the Instant Dict club.

BAMLETT, HERBERT

Herbert Bamlett made his name as a referee rather than as a player, his last match in charge being the FA Cup Final of 1914 between Burnley and Liverpool. This was the last Cup Final to be held at the Crystal Palace and the first to be honoured by the presence of the reigning monarch King George V.

Bamlett entered management with Oldham Athletic and in 1914–15, his first season with the club, he led them to runners-up spot in the First Division. Called up for military service in the summer of 1916, Bamlett faced the difficult task of reconstructing the team following his demobilization in February 1919. After two seasons of indifferent performances, Bamlett resigned to take charge of Wigan Borough's first season in the new Third Division (North).

In 1923 he joined Middlesbrough but after losing players of the calibre of Tim Williamson, the club suffered their first-ever relegation to Division Two. The club kept faith in Bamlett and in 1926–27, 'Boro won the Second Division Championship though rather surprisingly he was dismissed with the club on the verge of promotion!

Bamlett was appointed manager of Manchester United and stayed at Old Trafford for four seasons. In 1930–31 the club conceded 115 goals and were relegated after finishing bottom of the First Division.

BARMBY, NICK

The son of the old Hull City player Jeff Barmby, he joined Tottenham Hotspur in March 1990 before turning professional early the next year, having spent some time at the Lilleshall Centre of Excellence. After making his league debut at Sheffield Wednesday in September 1992, he scored on his home debut against Middlesbrough after coming on as a substitute.

He caused a club versus country row when he was selected for the England Youth side competing in the World Cup Finals in Australia. Even though Spurs wanted him to stay and help them during their FA Cup campaign, the FA got their way and he went to Australia. After helping England to third place, he returned to White Hart Lane in time for their losing FA Cup semi-final against Arsenal.

In the summer of 1995 he was surprisingly allowed to join

Middlesbrough for £5.25 million. He scored on his debut for the Riverside club in a 1–1 draw at Arsenal. Barmby went on to become 'Boro's leading scorer that season, albeit with seven goals, his form earning him a further eight caps for England at full international level, including three substitute appearances in Euro '96. Barmby, who had quickly established himself as a firm favourite at the new Holgate End had scored 10 goals in 49 games when he was sold to Everton for £5.75 million in October 1996 as Robson sought to strengthen his defence.

At Goodison Park, Barmby suffered with a recurrence of a long-standing groin injury but has now fully recovered. Still hugely popular among Everton supporters, he has now scored 23 goals in 135 games for the Merseyside club. Barmby was the surprise package in Kevin Keegan's Euro 2000 squad.

Nick Barmby

BAXTER, BOB

Middlesbrough manager Peter McWilliam spotted coal-miner Bob Baxter playing for Bruntonian Juniors whilst on a scouting mission to Scotland and brought him back to Ayresome Park where he made his debut in a 4–1 win at Birmingham in October 1932. Baxter was a first team regular with 'Boro for the next seven seasons, switching from inside-forward to centre-half following Tom Griffith's transfer to Aston Villa midway through the 1935–36 season.

Baxter, who showed his versatility by playing in nine different positions during his time at Ayresome Park, also captained the club, leading them to fourth in Division One in 1938–39, his last league season with 'Boro.

On the outbreak of the Second World War, Baxter, who had scored 20 goals in 266 League and Cup games returned to his native Scotland to resume his occupation as a coal miner. However, he still 'guested' for both Hibs and Hearts, joining the latter club on a permanent basis following his release from Middlesbrough in 1945. On his retirement from playing, he managed Leith Athletic before taking charge of the Edinburgh Monarchs speedway team.

BAXTER, MICK

Mick Baxter joined the staff of Preston North End shortly after his brother Stuart, also a central defender, had made his debut for the Deepdale club. After signing professional forms on his 18th birthday, he made his league debut against Grimsby Town in April 1975 and early the following season, he replaced his brother Stuart as the club's regular centre-half.

A powerful central defender, he went on to score 17 goals in 210 league games for North End before being transferred to Middlesbrough in August 1981 for a fee of £350,000.

Baxter made his debut for 'Boro in a 3–1 home defeat by Spurs on the opening day of the 1981–82 season and though he went on to play in 40 games that campaign, he couldn't prevent the club from losing its First Division status. He missed just one game in each of the following two seasons but after 138 appearances for the Ayresome Park club, he moved to Portsmouth.

Unfortunately he never played for Pompey due to illness and had to end his playing career. He returned to Deepdale as the club's Community Development Officer but sadly died in 1989, aged just 33.

BECK, MIKKEL

Danish international Mikkel Beck arrived at Middlesbrough on a free transfer from Fortuna Cologne in September 1996 after a legal wrangle with the German Second Division club.

He made his debut in a goalless home draw against Wimbledon and though the club lost their Premiership status at the end of the season, Beck had proved his worth as a goalscoring opportunist.

In 1997–98, Beck was the club's leading goalscorer with 14 goals as the club won promotion to the top flight at the first time of asking. The following season saw the Dane spend almost as much time on the substitute's bench than he did in a starting line-up. The hard-working forward was allowed to leave the Riverside Stadium in transfer deadline week, joining Jim Smith's Derby County for £500,000. The popular striker was an important member of the Rams' side, in 1999-2000, helping them retain their Premier League status.

BELL, HARRY

Harry Bell began his career with Hylton Colliery before signing for Sunderland on amateur forms in 1943. He stayed with the Roker Park club until September 1945 when 'Boro manager David Jack paid £1,250 for his services. After playing in 36 regional league games and the FA Cup competition of 1945–46, he made his Football League debut for 'Boro in a 1–0 win at Aston Villa on the first day league football was resumed.

Bell had arrived at Ayresome Park as an inside-forward but was successfully converted to right-half where over eight seasons of first team football he was one of the club's most consistent performers.

Bell went on to score 10 goals in 315 League and Cup games for 'Boro before leaving Ayresome Park to join Darlington. He appeared in 125 league games for the Quakers before hanging up his boots.

BELL, STEPHEN

Middlesbrough-born winger and England Youth international Stephen Bell began his league career with his home-town club and was only 16 years 323 days old when he made his debut in a 1–0 home defeat at the hands of Southampton in January 1982. It was his only appearance that season as 'Boro were relegated to the Second Division. The following campaign Bell was ever-present as 'Boro finished 16th in Division Two and scored eight goals, just one behind joint-top scorers Heine Otto and Duncan Shearer.

Following the departure of Malcolm Allison, who had great faith in

young Bell's ability, the youngster's appearances in the 'Boro first team became less frequent. He had scored 14 goals in 94 games for the Ayresome Park club when with Willie Maddren at the helm, Bell's contract was cancelled.

He drifted out of the professional game but in 1985, Alan Ball gave Bell the chance to resurrect his career with Portsmouth. Sadly, Bell walked out on the Fratton Park club and returned to the north-east where he later played in 40 league games for Darlington before hanging up his boots.

BEST STARTS
Middlesbrough were unbeaten for the first 10 games of the 1910–11 season. They won five and drew five of these matches before losing 4–2 at Bury on 12 November 1910. Despite this start, 'Boro won just two of their last 22 matches to finish 16th in Division One.

BIRKETT, RALPH
Ralph Birkett played junior football for Dartmouth United before joining Torquay United in 1929. He spent four years with his home-town club and scored 15 goals in 95 games for the Plainmoor club. In April 1933 he was transferred to Arsenal and in his first season with the club won a League Championship medal. Also in that 1933–34 season he won an FA Charity Shield medal after scoring twice in a 3–0 win over Everton. He had originally been signed to replace the ageing Joe Hulme but with Hulme resurrecting his career he was allowed to leave Highbury and joined Middlesbrough in March 1935 for a fee of £2,000.

He made his debut in a 2–0 defeat at Preston North End but then went on to score four goals in six appearances to help 'Boro retain their top flight status. In 1935–36, Birkett's early season form led to him winning full international honours for England against Northern Ireland in Belfast. That season he struck up a great goalscoring partnership with George Camsell and netted 22 goals from 36 games on the right-wing. Included in this total was a hat-trick in a 6–1 home win over Everton. His four years at Ayresome Park saw him mature into one of the finest right-wingers of the late 1930s but after scoring 36 goals in 101 games, he left to join Newcastle United for £6,000. Birkett retired from football during the Second World War.

BIRRELL, BILLY
Despite his experiences during the First World War when he suffered a

foot injury whilst serving with the Black Watch, he was later captured just before the Armistice was signed and spent the remaining weeks of the hostilities as a prisoner of war.

After the war he played for Raith Rovers but decided that after one season with the Scottish club, he would emigrate to America. He had completed all the necessary arrangements when 'Boro manager Jimmy Howie came in with an offer of £2,100 to take Birrell to Ayresome Park. Though he was still troubled by his war wound, he made his Middlesbrough debut in a 1–0 win at West Bromwich Albion. He was a first team regular at Ayresome Park for seven seasons, scoring 63 goals in 235 games including a hat-trick in a 5–3 defeat at Everton in February 1923.

Appointed club captain, he skippered 'Boro to the Second Division Championship in 1926–27 but midway through the following season he left the club to return to Raith Rovers as player-manager with Syd James joining 'Boro in an exchange deal.

In 1930, Birrell became secretary-manager of Bournemouth and five years later took over the reins at Queen's Park Rangers. By the outbreak of the Second World War, Birrell was managing Chelsea with his assistant being his former Middlesbrough colleague Stewart Davidson. After leading the Stamford Bridge club to two wartime finals, Birrell retired as manager in 1952.

BLACKMORE, CLAYTON

Welsh international Clayton Blackmore appeared in Manchester United's 1982 FA Youth Cup final side before making his league debut in the final game of the 1983–84 season at Nottingham Forest. Gradually he began to get more opportunities and in 1985–86 established himself as a first team regular in the United side. That season he won the first of 39 caps when he played for Wales against Norway.

With United he won a Premier League Championship medal and a European Cup Winners' Cup medal but in the summer of 1994 after playing in 249 games for United and scoring 27 goals, he joined Middlesbrough on a free transfer.

One of Bryan Robson's first signings, he made his 'Boro debut in a 2–0 home win over Burnley on the opening day of the 1994–95 season, helping the club to win the First Division Championship. Though his first team appearances got fewer with each passing season, Blackmore lent his vast experience to the club's reserve side, where he helped them

win the Pontin's League Second Division Championship. However, following a loan spell with Bristol City, he returned to the 'Boro side, winning an FA Cup runners-up medal in 1997.

Blackmore had scored four goals in 65 games for 'Boro when he was allowed to join former Middlesbrough favourites John Hendrie and Craig Hignett at Barnsley in February 1999.

BLOOMER, STEVE

Steve Bloomer was not only one of the greatest goalscorers of his time but was also one of the most enduring. He was just 17 when he first turned out for Derby County. Pale, thin, fragile, ghost-like, almost ill-looking, he caused the Derby crowd to laugh when they first caught sight of this most unlikely deadly striker. But they didn't laugh for long!

Fatty Foulke, the Sheffield United, Chelsea and England goalkeeper weighed in at around 20 stone for most of his career. With Foulke and his bulk seemingly covering most of the goal, he and Bloomer were inevitable rivals in the public eye. It was certainly a challenge to Bloomer's precision of shot. Despite the elephantine obstruction that appeared before him, Bloomer was more than often not the winner, although in their first vital clash in the 1899 FA Cup Final at Crystal Palace, Foulke was only beaten once and not by Bloomer as Derby lost 4–1. The previous season, Derby had lost their first final 3–1 to Nottingham Forest with Bloomer scoring their only goal.

It was John Goodall who had more influence on Steve Bloomer than any other player. It was Goodall, a former member of the Preston 'double' side who advised the England selectors to overlook him in order to give Bloomer his first cap.

Bloomer's international career was as distinguished as his league scoring feats, scoring 28 goals in just 23 internationals.

He left Derby in the middle of the 1906–07 season to join Middlesbrough, making his debut in a 6–1 defeat by Liverpool in March 1907. The following season he was the club's leading scorer with 20 goals including four in a 5–3 home win over Woolwich Arsenal. He was joint-top scorer in 1907–08 and in four seasons at Ayresome Park he made a great contribution to the club's efforts to maintain top flight status. He had scored 62 goals in 130 games for 'Boro when in September 1910 he returned to play for Derby County. In 1911–12 he captained the Rams to promotion from the Second Division and took his tally of goals for Derby to 332 in 525 League and Cup games.

In 1914 he went to coach in Germany but was interned for the duration of the First World War. When the hostilities were over he returned to the Baseball Ground as the club's general assistant. Later dogged by ill-health he was sent on a cruise but sadly died just three weeks after returning home.

BOAM, STUART

One of Middlesbrough's most successful captains, Stuart Boam began his Football League career with Mansfield Town. He missed very few games in his four seasons at Field Mill, playing in 170 league games, 162 of them consecutively.

In May 1971, Boam left the Stags to join Middlesbrough for £50,000 and made his debut in a 2–1 defeat at Portsmouth on the opening day of the 1971–72 season.

Stuart Boam

Following Jack Charlton's arrival as manager in the summer of 1973, Boam was made club captain, developing a fine understanding at the heart of the 'Boro defence with Willie Maddren. In 1973–74 he was ever-present as the club won the Second Division Championship.

Boam missed very few games for Middlesbrough in eight seasons at Ayresome Park but fell out with John Neal when he replaced Charlton as 'Boro boss. Boam decided to relinquish the role of first team captain but Neal soon had a change of heart and restored him to the role of skipper. However, just before the start of the 1979–80 season, Boam, who had scored 16 goals in 393 games was allowed to leave Ayresome Park and joined rivals Newcastle United for £100,000.

Boam made 77 first team appearances for the Magpies before leaving St James Park to return to Mansfield Town as player-manager. He later played a few games for Fourth Division Hartlepool United before entering non-League football as player-manager of Guisborough Town.

BRAWN, BILLY

After playing his early football with his home-town club, Wellingborough Town, Billy Brawn played for Northampton Town and Sheffield United before signing for Aston Villa in December 1901.

At 6ft 1ins and 13st 5lbs, he was tall and heavy for a winger but he won two England caps in 1904 and an FA Cup winners' medal in 1905 before leaving Villa Park the following year to play for Middlesbrough.

His first game for the club was in a 1–0 home defeat by Sheffield United, one of his former clubs. Despite that setback, Brawn helped 'Boro to win four of their last six games and so preserve their First Division status. One of the leading players of the day, Brawn's stay at Ayresome Park was brief and after appearing in 58 games he left to play for Chelsea and later Brentford where he subsequently became a director.

BROTHERS

The only set of brothers to play for Middlesbrough have been the Carrs. The eldest, centre-half Willie Carr, joined the club in November 1910 along with centre-forward Henry and they were followed early the following year by Jackie. Later at the end of the First World War, younger brother George also joined the Ayresome Park club. The most famous of the brothers was Jackie Carr who scored 81 goals in 449 games over 16 seasons with the club. Willie Carr made 118 appearances for the club whilst Harry scored three goals in the three games he played for 'Boro

in the 1910–11 season. George Carr scored 23 goals in 70 games for the club including two hat-tricks in 1921–22 as 'Boro beat Aston Villa (Home 5–0) and Bolton Wanderers (Home 4–2).

There were never any occasions when all four brothers played in the same team but there were 15 matches when Willie, Jackie and George all played in the same Middlesbrough side.

BROWN, BILLY

Billy Brown, who worked as a miner, played part-time football for West Stanley before joining Middlesbrough in December 1928.

Despite a series of outstanding performances in the club's reserve team, it was another three years before he made his first team debut. That came in August 1931 as 'Boro drew 2–2 at Leicester City, after which he established himself as a first team regular for the next eight seasons.

Brown, who played his early games for the club at wing-half, switched to right-back following an injury to Jack Jennings. He went on to play in 273 League and Cup games for 'Boro up until the outbreak of the Second World War during which he 'guested' for Watford.

He left Ayresome Park at the end of the 1945–46 season to sign for Hartlepool United. He appeared in 80 league games for the then Third Division (North) club before hanging up his boots.

BRUCE, BOBBY

Glasgow-born forward Bobby Bruce joined Aberdeen from local club St Anthony's and after impressing in the Dons' reserve side won a regular place in the Pittodrie club's first team. A prolific goalscorer in Scottish League football, he once netted a hat-trick for the Dons in a Scottish Cup tie but was still on the losing side.

Bruce joined Middlesbrough for a fee of £4,500 midway through the 1927–28 season and made his debut in a 5–2 defeat at Bolton Wanderers. The following season he scored 11 goals in 35 games as 'Boro won the Second Division Championship. The scorer of a number of spectacular goals for the club, his powerful shooting and eye for goal led to him winning full international honours for Scotland in November 1933 when he played against Austria.

Bruce had scored 71 goals in 253 League and Cup games when he was transferred to Sheffield Wednesday in October 1935 for £2,500. His stay at Hillsborough was brief and in the summer of 1936 he joined Ipswich Town. He later played non-League football for Mossley.

BURNS, MICKY

A former England amateur international, he played non-League football for Chorley and Skelmersdale United before joining Blackpool. A fast winger who could also score goals, he found the net on his league debut as the Seasiders beat Portsmouth 2–1 on the opening day of the 1969–70 season. That campaign saw the Bloomfield Road club win promotion to the First Division but though Burns was top-scorer in 1970–71, the Lancashire club were relegated. Burns' best season for Blackpool was 1971–72 when he top-scored with 20 goals including netting a hat-trick in a 5–0 home win over Watford. Also that season he scored four goals in a 10–0 Anglo-Italian Cup win over Lanerossi Vicenza. He had scored 62 goals in 203 games for the Seasiders when in the summer of 1974 he left to play for Newcastle United.

Micky Burns

In his first season at St James Park, he won a Texaco Cup winners' medal and in 1976 he played in the League Cup Final. On leaving the Magpies he became player-coach of Cardiff City but was unable to settle in South Wales and in October 1979 he joined Middlesbrough for £72,000.

His first game in 'Boro's colours saw him score one of the club's goals in a 3–2 defeat at Manchester United but a back injury restricted his appearances later in the campaign. Over the next two seasons, Burns took his tally of goals for the club to 24 in 67 League and Cup games before coaching the club's juniors. After losing his job as part of 'Boro's economy drive, he became the PFA's education officer.

C

CAMSELL, GEORGE

The scorer of a record 59 league goals when Middlesbrough won the Second Division Championship in 1926–27, George Camsell joined the Ayresome Park club from Durham City in October 1925 for a fee of £600. After making his debut in a 1–0 home win over Nottingham Forest, Camsell lost form and though he scored three goals in his four appearances that season, he almost left the club to play for Barnsley.

His career at Ayresome Park began to flourish after he came into the side for the fifth game of the 1926–27 season, helping them to win nine of their next ten games. Camsell scored 29 goals in 12 consecutive games for the club, ending the campaign with 59 goals. After scoring all five goals in a 5–3 win at Manchester City, he netted four goals in the wins over Portsmouth (Home 7–3) Fulham (Home 6–1) and Swansea Town (Home 7–1) and hat-tricks against Notts County (Home 4–2) Port Vale (Home 5–2) Grimsby Town (Away 7–4) South Shields (Home 5–0) and Reading (Home 5–0). Not surprisingly 'Boro won promotion to the top flight as Second Division champions.

Camsell also proved himself to be a prolific goalscorer at international level and his total of 18 goals in nine internationals included four in a 5–1 win over Belgium and a hat-trick in a 6–0 defeat of Wales.

Though Middlesbrough were relegated after just one season in the First Division, Camsell still scored 33 goals in 40 games including four goals in the wins over Everton (Home 4–2) and Bury (Home 6–1).

He won another Second Division Championship medal with 'Boro in 1928–29, his total of 30 goals including hat-tricks against Wolves (Home 8–3) and Clapton Orient (Home 4–0). He continued to score at a terrific rate for the next ten seasons, taking his tally of goals for 'Boro to 345 in 453 League and Cup games.

On hanging up his boots, Camsell remained at Ayresome Park, working as the club's chief scout, coach and assistant-secretary.

CAPACITY
The total capacity of the Riverside Stadium in 1999-2000 was 35,000.

CAPS (ENGLAND)
The first Middlesbrough player to be capped by England was Alf Common when he played against Wales in 1906. The most capped player is Wilf Mannion with 26 caps.

CAPS (NORTHERN IRELAND)
The first Middlesbrough player to be capped by Northern Ireland was Joe Miller when he played against Wales in 1929. The most capped player is Eric McMordie with 21 caps.

CAPS (REPUBLIC OF IRELAND)
The first Middlesbrough player to be capped by the Republic of Ireland was Jimmy Hartnett when he played against Spain in 1949. The most capped player is Arthur Fitzsimons with 25 caps.

CAPS (SCOTLAND)
The first Middlesbrough player to be capped by Scotland was Archie Brown when he played against England in 1904. The most capped players are Jock Marshall, Derek Whyte and Andy Wilson, each with six caps.

CAPS (WALES)
The first Middlesbrough player to be capped by Wales was Ben Lewis when he played against Scotland in 1893. The most capped player is John Mahoney with 13 caps.

CAPTAINS
Among the many players who have captained the club are Billy Birrell who skippered 'Boro to the Second Division Championship in 1926–27.

That season he missed just one game as the club finished eight points ahead of runners-up Portsmouth. One of the club's best-ever captains was Bob Baxter, a great utility player who appeared in 266 games for Middlesbrough. Unfortunately he never captained the club to League or Cup success. George Hardwick captained England in each of his 13 full international appearances. During his time as 'Boro captain he once won the toss in the FA Cup third round tie against Brentford at Griffin Park on 8 January 1949 and chose to select the way his team would play. However, Micky Fenton 'Boro's centre-forward kicked off and the game was in progress before anyone noticed the mistake!

Long-serving Gordon Jones was Middlesbrough captain when the club won promotion from the Third Division in 1966–67 and Stuart Boam skippered the club's Second Division Championship winning side of 1973–74.

One of the most respected captains in the club's history was Tony Mowbray who skippered the club to successive promotions at the end of the 1980s and led 'Boro out at Wembley in the final of the Zenith Data Systems Final in 1990.

Boro's captain in recent seasons has been Nigel Pearson, a truly inspirational leader. Known by the fans as 'Captain Fantastic', he has seen 'Boro promoted, relegated and appear at Wembley in three finals.

CARR, GEORGE

One of five footballing brothers, George Carr began his career with Bradford Park Avenue in 1916, signing for 'Boro in the summer of 1919. His first game for the club came in November 1919 as 'Boro lost 5–3 at Aston Villa with George Elliott netting all three of Middlesbrough's goals. Carr's best season for the club in terms of goals scored was 1921–22 when he netted 15 in 28 league games. His total included two hat-tricks against Aston Villa (Home 5–0) and Bolton Wanderers (Home 4–2). He had scored 23 goals in 70 games when he left Ayresome Park to join Leicester City.

At Filbert Street he showed his versatility and scored the goal against Bradford City which guaranteed the club's promotion to the top flight in 1924–25. Having arrived at the club as an inside-forward he switched to centre-half with great success and was the lynch-pin on which Leicester launched a series of near misses on the League Championship. After scoring 25 goals in 192 games, he left the Foxes to end his career with Stockport County. He later played non-League football for Nuneaton Borough before managing Cheltenham Town.

In later years he helped to initiate the fostering of Middlesbrough Swifts as a Leicester City nursery team before coaching both Stockton and South Bank.

CARR, JACKIE

Probably the most famous of the footballing brothers, Jackie Carr began his career with South Bank and in 1910 he helped them reach the FA Amateur Cup Final where they lost to the Royal Marine Light Infantry at Bishop Auckland. Shortly afterwards, he joined Middlesbrough and made his debut on 2 January 1911, scoring both goals in a 2–2 draw with Nottingham Forest. It was 1912–13 before he won a regular place in the 'Boro side, scoring 19 goals in 34 games. Included in this total, his best in 16 seasons football for the Ayresome Park club was a hat-trick in a 4–1 FA Cup replay win over Millwall. His only other hat-trick for the club also came in the FA Cup when 'Boro beat Goole Town 9–3 in 1914–15.

During the First World War, Carr served in the Royal Engineers and when league football resumed in 1919–20 his form was such that he was capped by England against Ireland at Belfast and had an impressive game in a 1–1 draw. He won another cap against Wales in 1923 but then contracted pneumonia. Thankfully he recovered and in 1926–27 and 1928–29 helped 'Boro win the Second Division Championship.

He went on to score 81 goals in 449 League and Cup games for Middlesbrough before leaving to join Blackpool. After helping the Seasiders win promotion to the First Division, he left Bloomfield Road to become player-coach at Hartlepool United. He later managed the Victoria Park club and also had spells in charge at both Tranmere Rovers and Darlington.

CARTER, RAICH

His father was 'Toddler' Carter, a winger with Port Vale, Fulham and Southampton who sadly died of a brian tumour when Raich was just 14, having never seen his son play.

Raich Carter caught the selector's eye early and after appearing for Sunderland Boys, played in the same distinguished England Schoolboys team as Len Goulden and Cliff Bastin.

After leaving school, he became an errand boy and then apprentice electrician but his heart was not in electrical engineering and he jumped at the chance of a trial with Leicester City. Told that he was too small

for professional football, he decided to seek a trial with Sunderland and though he signed amateur forms for the Wearsiders he was not used again after his trial. Forgetting that he was still technically on Sunderland's books, he was given the chance of a trial with Huddersfield Town. This led to a row between the managers of the two clubs but gave Carter his chance. He played a number of games in Sunderland's reserves before being offered professional terms.

He made his league debut in a 3–1 defeat at Sheffield Wednesday in October 1932 and two games later scored his first goal for the club in a 7–4 win over Bolton Wanderers. In 1933–34 he netted his first hat-trick for the Wearsiders in a 6–0 win over Spurs, his form leading to him winning the first of 13 full caps for England. Appointed the club's captain, he led Sunderland to the League Championship in 1935–36, scoring 31 goals in 39 games, including four goals in a 6–1 defeat of West Bromwich Albion. The following season he scored another hat-trick in a 4–1 win over Middlesbrough and led Sunderland to their first-ever FA Cup Final triumph.

After bomb damage to the family home, Carter moved to Derby where he played his wartime football. He joined the Rams on a permanent basis and won another FA Cup medal, the only player to win such a medal before and after the war.

On leaving the Baseball Ground, he stepped down to the Third Division with Hull City and almost immediately found himself player-manager as Tigers' boss Frank Buckley moved on. After a short spell with Cork Athletic, Carter became manager of Leeds United before taking charge at Mansfield Town.

In January 1963 he became manager of Middlesbrough following the departure of Bob Dennison. Unfortunately his days at Ayresome Park were without doubt the least successful of a long and distinguished career. In February 1966 with the club on the brink of relegation to the Third Division for the first time in its history, he was dismissed.

CENTURIES

There are seven instances of individual players who have scored 100 or more league goals for Middlesbrough. George Camsell is the greatest goalscorer with 325 strikes in his 'Boro career (1925–1939). Other centurions are George Elliott (203), Brian Clough (197), John Hickton (159), Micky Fenton (147), Alan Peacock (125), and Bernie Slaven (118).

David Armstrong holds the club record for the most consecutive

league appearances with 305. Other players to have made over 100 consecutive appearances during their careers are Ray Yeoman (190), Bernie Slaven (136), Tim Williamson (130), Bill Harris (129), Willie Maddren (125), Gary Pallister (117), Tony Mowbray (111), and Stuart Boam (105).

CHADWICK, DAVID

David Chadwick graduated through Southampton's junior sides and in October 1959, aged 16 years 2 months, he became the youngest player to turn out for the reserves. His early promise did not develop as Saints had hoped and over the next six seasons, he struggled to gain a first team place.

In July 1966, Middlesbrough paid £10,000 to take Chadwick to Ayresome Park and he made his debut in a 3–2 win at Colchester United on the opening day of the 1966–67 season. That campaign he missed just two games as 'Boro won promotion to the Second Division. Though he only scored two goals, the tricky winger's strikes came in the space of five days over Christmas, enabling the club to pick up valuable points against Darlington (Away 3–0) and Bristol Rovers (Away 2–2). In 1967–68 Chadwick continued to be an important member of the Middlesbrough side but early the following season he lost out to Derek Downing and in January 1970 after scoring four goals in 116 games he was sold to Halifax Town.

He scored 15 goals in 95 league games for the Shaymen before returning to the south coast to play for Bournemouth. After a loan spell at Torquay United he ended his league career with Gillingham after appearing in 294 games for his six clubs.

CHAMPIONSHIPS

Middlesbrough have won a divisional championship on four occasions. The club won the Second Division title in 1926–27, despite losing their first three games of the season. Their first point came in a goalless draw at South Shields before they won their next six matches. After losing 4–3 at Nottingham Forest, 'Boro lost just one of their next 25 matches. During this spell they scored seven goals on three occasions - Portsmouth (Home 7–3), Swansea Town (Home 7–1) and Grimsby Town (Away 7–4). They ended the season scoring 122 goals, a club record and finished with 62 points, eight more than runners-up Portsmouth. The hero of the season was George Camsell who netted 59 goals.

'Boro's stay in the top flight was brief for in 1927–28 they finished

bottom of the First Division and were relegated. They bounced back at the first attempt, winning the Second Division Championship for the second time in three years. This time they totalled 55 points with their biggest win being an 8–3 defeat of Wolverhampton Wanderers. Billy Pease scored four of the goals and George Camsell who top-scored with 30 goals, a hat-trick.

'Boro's third Championship success came in 1973–74 when they again won the Second Division title. After winning 1–0 at Portsmouth on the opening day of the season, 'Boro lost 2–0 at home to Fulham. They then lost just one match (Nottingham Forest Away 1–5) out of the next 36, including a run of nine successive victories to win the Championship with eight matches still to play! The season had seen the club establish a number of records including their highest total of points, 65, a run of 20 home games without defeat and an unbeaten league run of 24 games.

The club's last Championship success was in 1994–95 when with Bryan Robson at the helm, they won the First Division title. Unbeaten until the eighth match of the campaign, 'Boro continued to pick up the points and ended the year five points clear of second placed Wolves. The New Year saw 'Boro in unconvincing form as a run of four matches without a win cost them top place. New signing Uwe Fuchs from Kaiserslautern scored some important goals including a hat-trick against Bristol City and along with another signing Jan Aage Fjortoft from Swindon, strengthened 'Boro's position at the top. Despite the club's end of season form being less impressive, all of the challengers also slipped up and after beating Luton Town 2–1, 'Boro were crowned champions.

CHARLTON, JACK

In a long playing career at Leeds United, Jack Charlton made 629 appearances, scoring 70 goals, mainly from free-kicks and corners. His career at Elland Road was overshadowed by his brother Bobby at Manchester United but after John Charles' departure to Juventus, Jack's career came into its own. Under Don Revie he developed into a fine centre-half, winning 35 caps for England and a World Cup winners' medal in 1966. After Leeds United gained promotion as champions of the Second Division in 1964, honours came thick and fast and in 1967 he was voted Footballer of the Year. He retired from playing in 1973 when he was offered the manager's job at Middlesbrough.

By the end of his first season in charge at Ayresome Park, 'Boro had won the Second Division Championship. After establishing themselves in the top flight, they reached the semi-finals of the League Cup and won the Anglo-Scottish Cup. However, on 21 April 1977, Charlton resigned after four years in charge at Ayresome Park. He felt that he needed a six-month break from the game. When he resigned, Charlton said 'I have not known anything but football and felt that I needed a change, made my decision and went.'

Charlton returned to football in October 1977 as manager of Sheffield Wednesday. They had just gone ten games without a win and looked to be heading for Fourth Division football but Charlton led the club to a respectable mid-table position. It wasn't long before Charlton created a team which won promotion to Division Two in 1979–80. Two years

Jack Charlton

later, Wednesday missed further promotion to the top flight by one point.

However, in 1983 just after the Owls had reached the FA Cup semi-finals, Charlton resigned. After a brief spell as caretaker-manager of Middlesbrough, he took control at Newcastle United but it was an unhappy time for the big Geordie and after being barracked by the crowd, he resigned in August 1985. In February 1986 he was appointed by the Irish FA to take over the running of the national side on a part-time basis. In 1988 the Republic of Ireland reached the European Championship finals for the first time and in 1990, the World Cup Finals, where they lost 1–0 to Italy in the quarter-finals. Though he led the Irish to the 1994 World Cup finals, they went out to Holland in the second round. In 1995–96 he stepped down to be replaced by Mick McCarthy.

CLEAN SHEETS

This is the colloquial expression used to describe a goalkeeper's performance when he does not concede a goal. Stephen Pears in 1986–87 kept 27 clean sheets from 46 league appearances to help 'Boro finish runners-up in the Third Division. Pears also kept a further three clean sheets in the club's FA Cup and League Cup matches.

CLOUGH, BRIAN

One of nine children, Brian Clough worked as a clerk with ICI whilst playing for Billingham Synthonia and Great Broughton before joining Middlesbrough. He made his debut in a 1–1 draw at home to Barnsley in September 1955 when the club were in the middle of an injury crisis. It was the following season before Clough established himself in the Middlesbrough side, top-scoring with 40 goals in 44 games including four in a 7–2 home win over Huddersfield Town and a hat-trick in a 4–0 win at Nottingham Forest. Clough continued to find the back of the net in 1957–58, his total of 42 goals including four in the matches against Doncaster Rovers (Home 5–0) and Ipswich Town (Home 5–2) and a hat-trick in a 5–1 home win over Grimsby Town.

Clough who headed the Second Division goalscoring charts for three consecutive seasons, netted 43 goals in 1958–59 including five in the 9–0 rout of Brighton and Hove Albion on the opening day of the season. He also scored four goals in the 6–2 win over Swansea and hat-tricks against Scunthorpe United (Home 6–1 and Away 3–0) and Brighton (Away 6–4).

Over these three seasons, Clough had put in numerous transfer requests, all of which were turned down. However, in November 1959, a month after he won two full caps for England, a number of his team-mates signed a petition asking for him to be released of the captaincy! It didn't affect Clough, he still scored 40 goals in 42 games including four in a 6–2 defeat of Plymouth Argyle and hat-tricks in the wins over Charlton Athletic (Home 3–0), Bristol Rovers (Home 5–1), Stoke City (Away 5–2), and Bristol City (Home 6–3).

Clough's last season at Ayresome Park was 1960–61 when he failed for the first time to pass the 40 goal mark. His total of 36 goals in 42 games included his 16th and 17th hat-tricks for the club in the 6–6 draw against Charlton Athletic and the 3–0 win at Portsmouth. Clough, who had scored 204 goals in 222 games was eventually allowed to leave Ayresome Park and in the summer of 1961 joined Sunderland for £45,000.

He scored 63 goals in 74 games for Sunderland before an injury he received against Bury on Boxing Day 1962 virtually ended his playing career. After a spell on Sunderland's coaching staff he took his first steps in management with Hartlepool United. He turned the club's fortunes around, building a squad that was to gain promotion at the end of the 1967–68 season. But by then, Clough and his partner Peter Taylor had moved to Derby County. After helping the Rams win the Second Division Championship in 1970–71 they led them to the League Championship the following season and in 1972–73 to the semi-finals of the European Cup. In October 1973, Clough left the Baseball Ground to manage Brighton before taking over at Leeds United in the summer of 1974. Sacked after only 44 days in charge, he was not out of work for long and in January 1975 was appointed manager of Nottingham Forest. Over the next 18 years he was to produce some golden moments for Forest, including a League Championship, four League Cup wins and two European Cup successes. There is no doubt that Brian Clough was one of the greatest managers of all-time. He decided to retire in May 1993 amidst a lot of bad publicity, having won just about everything there is to win.

COCHRANE, TERRY

After unimpressive trials with both Nottingham Forest and Everton, Terry Cochrane seemed to have missed his chance of succeeding in the professional game. He had played part-time with Derry and Linfield

before joining Coleraine whom he helped to victory in the Irish Cup Final of 1975. Shortly afterwards he won his first full cap for Northern Ireland against Norway in Belfast.

In October 1976, Burnley manager Joe Brown paid £38,000 for his services. Though he scored on his debut, he spent two relatively undistinguished years at Turf Moor. He was transferred to Middlesbrough soon after the start of the 1978–79 season and made his debut in a 2–0 home win over Norwich City.

During his five years at Ayresome Park, Cochrane proved to be a great crowd favourite with his great ball control and dazzling wing play. Whilst with 'Boro he won a further 19 caps for Northern Ireland but in 1982 he was unable to prevent the club being relegated back to Division Two. After scoring 12 goals in 128 games and amid rumours of a rift

Terry Cochrane

with 'Boro manager Malcolm Allison, he moved to Third Division Gillingham.

In each of his three seasons at the Priestfield Stadium, the Gills flirted with promotion but in 1986 he left to try indoor football in Dallas. On his return to these shores he had brief spells with Millwall and Hartlepool United before playing for Billingham Synthonia in the Northern League and helping them win the Championship in 1988–89.

COLOURS

Following their formation in 1875, the club's first colours were red and black stripes but by the turn of the century they had changed to red shirts with a white yoke, a style which has re-appeared throughout the club's history. Though 'Boro's strip has often changed, it has virtually retained the shoulder-yoke format. The club' present colours are red and white whilst the change colours are white and purple.

COMMON, ALF

Alf Common started his footballing career playing junior football with South Hylton and Jarrow before joining his home-town club Sunderland in 1900. He won a regular place in the Sunderland side of 1901 when he helped them to the runners-up position in the First Division. With the Wearsiders having a surplus of inside-forwards, he was allowed to join Sheffield United for £325. In his first season with the Bramall Lane club he became a folk hero by scoring the winning goal in the 1902 FA Cup Final against Southampton. He stayed at Bramall Lane for a further two seasons in which time he won the first of his three England caps against Ireland in February 1904. He moved back to Sunderland for the start of the 1904–05 season before making football history by becoming the first-ever player to be transferred for a four-figure sum - £1,000, when he joined Middlesbrough in February 1905.

He made his debut at Sheffield United, scoring the only goal of the game from the penalty-spot to give 'Boro a 1–0 win. In 1905–06 Common was the club's top scorer with 24 goals, netting hat-tricks against Stoke (Home 5–0) and Brighton and Hove Albion at Bramall Lane in an FA Cup replay which 'Boro won 3–1. Forming a good striking partnership with Steve Bloomer, he scored another hat-trick for the club in a 4–2 win at Liverpool in April 1907. Early the following season he lost the Middlesbrough captaincy following 'drunkenness and violent behaviour' and three years later after scoring 65 goals in 178

games joined Woolwich Arsenal for £250. In 1911–12 he was the club's leading scorer but shortly afterwards he left to play for Preston North End, helping the Deepdale club win the Second Division Championship in his first season with the Lilywhites.

CONSECUTIVE HOME GAMES

Middlesbrough played an extraordinary sequence of five home games in succession during the promotion winning season of 1901–02 with the following results:

Date	Opposition	Score
28.12.1901	Blackpool	Won 2–1
01.01.1902	Burton United	Won 5–0
04.01.1902	Stockport County	Won 6–0
18.01.1902	Glossop	Won 5–0
01.02.1902	Lincoln City	Drew 0–0

CONSECUTIVE SCORING - LONGEST SEQUENCE

George Camsell holds the club record for consecutive scoring when he was on target in 12 consecutive league games. The sequence started when he scored in the 4–3 defeat at Nottingham Forest on 16 October 1926 and ended with a hat-trick in a 5–2 win over Port Vale at Ayresome Park on New Year's Day 1927. During the sequence Camsell scored all five goals in a 5–3 win at Manchester City and four goals in the wins over Portsmouth (Home 7–3), Fulham (Home 6–1), and Swansea Town (Home 7–1) and totalled 29 goals in the 12 games.

COOPER, COLIN

Middlesbrough-born defender Colin Cooper joined his home-town team on a YTS scheme, progressing through the ranks to make his league debut as a substitute for Don O'Riordan in a 2–1 defeat at Crystal Palace in March 1986. By the start of the following season, Cooper had won a regular place at left-back in the 'Boro side and was ever-present as the club won the Third Division Championship. He missed just one game in 1987–88 as 'Boro won promotion to the top flight. Predominantly right-footed he was switched to right-back when Jimmy Phillips arrived at the club. Unfortunately he was hampered by stress fractures to his right foot and was forced to miss a number of games at the end of the club's relegation season of 1988–89.

Following the appointment of Lennie Lawrence as Middlesbrough's manager, Cooper found his days at Ayresome Park numbered and after scoring nine goals in 239 games he was signed by Millwall boss Bruce Rioch for £300,000. It was Rioch's successor, current Republic of Ireland manager Mick McCarthy who was responsible for converting Cooper into a centre-back and after a number of impressive performances at the heart of the Millwall defence, Forest manager Frank Clark paid £1.5 million to take him to the City Ground.

In 1995, Cooper won two caps at full international level to go with the eight he had won for the England Under-21 side whilst with 'Boro. Following Stuart Pearce's departure from the City Ground, Cooper was appointed as club captain. Surprisingly, Forest accepted a £2.5 million offer from West Ham United for his services but Cooper refused to move. He had made 213 appearances for Forest before rejoining Middlesbrough for £2.5 million in the summer of 1998.

Strong and fearless in the tackle, Cooper has now taken his total of appearances to 301 in his two spells with the club.

COOPER, TERRY

Terry Cooper began his Football League career with Leeds United, making his first team debut on the day the club gained promotion to Division One in 1964. When he arrived at Elland Road he was a pacey left-winger but was soon switched to full-back with devastating effect. Eventually displacing Willie Bell he put his experience as a winger to good effect with breathtaking runs, adding weight to the Leeds attack. Although his goals were all too rare, he did score against Arsenal in the 1968 League Cup Final to give United their first major trophy. A couple of years later he won the first of 20 full caps for England and played in the 1970 World Cup. Cooper, who broke his leg at Stoke in 1972, played in 349 games for Leeds before joining Middlesbrough in March 1975 for a fee of £50,000.

His first game in 'Boro's colours came in a 3–0 home win over Tottenham Hotspur and he was a virtual ever-present over the next three seasons. His only goal for Middlesbrough came in a 2–0 win at Liverpool in March 1976 but two years later after appearing in 133 games, his 'Boro career came to an end when he refused to go on a tour to Norway. He was suspended by the club and after demanding a transfer joined his former Leeds United colleague Norman Hunter at Bristol City.

After just one season at Ashton Gate, he moved across the city to

Eastville where he became player-manager of Bristol Rovers. Controversially dismissed, Cooper returned to Yorkshire to team-up with another former Leeds player Billy Bremner at Doncaster Rovers. He later returned to Bristol City as player-manager, helping the Robins to two Wembley finals in the Freight Rover Trophy. On joining the board at Ashton Gate, he became Britain's first player-director before moving on to Exeter City. In August 1991 he became manager of Birmingham City before returning to St James Park for a second spell as Exeter boss. Cooper is now at the Dell where he is one of three joint-assistant managers.

COX, NEIL

After playing in only 17 league games for his home-town club, Scunthorpe United, Neil Cox was signed by Aston Villa manager Jozef Venglos on the recommendation of youth coach, Richard Money. Villa paid a staggering £400,000 for a player with less than six months Football League experience. Cox had to wait more than a year before making his first team debut at Notts County. Used mainly as full-back cover for Earl Barrett or in midfield, he never let the side down. Chosen for the England Under-21 side, he progressed well and played in 57 games for Villa before in July 1994, he became Middlesbrough's first £1 million player. He made his debut in a 2–0 home win over Burnley on the opening day of the 1994–95 season, at the end of which he had played in 40 league games, scoring his first goal in a 3–1 defeat of Swindon Town to help 'Boro win the First Division Championship. After that he was a virtual ever-present, occasionally deputising in the centre of the 'Boro defence, following Nigel Pearson's enforced absence through injury. Cox played in 128 games for 'Boro before following the club's disastrous 1996–97 season, he left to join Colin Todd's Bolton Wanderers for a fee of £1.2 million.

The Lancashire club had just returned to the Premier League but after just two appearances, he sustained a leg injury which kept him out for over half the 1997–98 season. On his return to the side he scored his first goal for the club against Aston Villa but it wasn't enough to save Bolton from relegation. In 1998–99, Cox had his best campaign for the club, his wholehearted displays making him a great favourite with the Bolton fans. He had played in 75 games for the Wanderers before leaving to play for Watford.

CRAGGS, JOHN

A former England Youth international, right-back John Craggs began his

league career with Newcastle United but after making just 52 League and Cup appearances in six years at St James Park, he was happy to move to Middlesbrough in the summer of 1971 when Jack Charlton paid £60,000 for his services.

Craggs made his 'Boro debut in a 2–1 home win over Sheffield Wednesday in the fourth match of the 1971–72 season after which he missed just one game in the rest of the campaign. Craggs was a first team regular for the Ayresome Park club for the next 10 seasons, being ever-present in 1976–77 and 1979–80.

One of the best attacking full-backs in the country, he scored some spectacular goals, perhaps none better than the strike that was good enough for 'Boro to beat Carlisle United at Ayresome Park during their Second Division Championship winning season of 1973–74.

Craggs went on to score 14 goals in 488 games for 'Boro before returning to St James Park on a free transfer. After taking his total of appearances in his two spells with the Magpies to 73, he joined Darlington where he later ended his playing career. In December 1988 Craggs left the Feethams to become youth team coach with Hartlepool United.

John Craggs

CRICKETERS

Whilst the club have had a number of accomplished cricketers, 'Boro's only first-class players have been Victor Fox and Alan Ramage. Victor Fox appeared in 112 games for 'Boro before leaving to play for Wolverhampton Wanderers. He played first-class cricket for Worcestershire and in 163 matches at county level, scored 6,654 runs at an average of 26.62.

Alan Ramage who appeared in 80 games for 'Boro and later played for Derby County, turned out for Yorkshire, scoring 53 runs at 17.66 and capturing 19 wickets at 30.15 runs apiece.

CROSSAN, JOHNNY

Born in Londonderry, Johnny Crossan played Irish League football for Derry City and Coleraine before problems over a proposed move to Bristol City resulted in a 'life' suspension and a move instead to Sparta Rotterdam. It was with Standard Liege that his skills were brought to a wider stage when he played for the Belgian champions in the European Cup.

When the ban was lifted, Crossan signed for Sunderland for £27,000 and helped the Wearsiders win promotion to the First Division. In January 1965 he moved to Manchester City for £40,000. Appointed captain of the Maine Road side, he helped them regain their First Division status and had scored 28 goals in 110 games when he was allowed to join Middlesbrough in August 1967 for a record fee of £35,000.

The Northern Ireland international made his debut in a 2–2 draw at Carlisle United in the second game of the 1967–68 season. Midway through the following campaign he began to suffer from insomnia but after receiving hospital treatment he had to undergo major abdominal surgery. Not surprisingly his form thereafter wasn't up to scratch and he was allowed to leave Ayresome Park and return to Belgium to play for Tongren FC.

CUMMING, DAVE

Goalkeeper Dave Cumming began his career with Aberdeen in 1929 but after four seasons at Pittodrie he was given a free transfer and left to join Arbroath. His performances for the Gayfield Park side led to a number of top clubs vying for his signature but it was Middlesbrough who secured his services for a fee of £3,000 in October 1936.

The most expensive 'keeper to come south of the border, he made his debut for 'Boro in a 3–3 home draw against Liverpool. He went on to

keep 10 clean sheets in 32 games to help 'Boro finish seventh in Division One. Cumming missed very few games in the seasons leading up to the Second World War, helping the club finish fifth in 1937–38 and fourth in 1938–39. His performances led to him being capped by Scotland against England at Wembley in 1938, a match Scotland won 1–0.

During the war years he 'guested' for Newcastle United but still managed to appear in 125 games for Middlesbrough. He was still the club's first-choice 'keeper when league football resumed in 1946–47 but when 'Boro played Arsenal at Highbury in April 1947 he was sent-off for striking the Gunners' Leslie Compton. The last of his 157 appearances came later that month as 'Boro were beaten 2–1 at home by Blackpool, a match in which he dislocated his kneecap.

D

DAVIDSON, STEWART

Right-half Stewart Davidson joined Middlesbrough from his home-town club Aberdeen in April 1913 for a fee of £675. His first game in 'Boro's colours was against Manchester City at Hyde Road on the opening day of the 1913–14 season, a game which ended all-square at 1–1. He went on to appear in 30 games that season, scoring in the 4–0 win over Liverpool and helping 'Boro finish third in Division One.

During the First World War, Davidson 'guested' for Chelsea but was later wounded in action. Thankfully by the time league football resumed in 1919–20 he was fully recovered and was the club's only ever-present. Davidson replaced George Elliott as the club's captain, his form winning him full international honours when he played for Scotland against England at Hampden Park.

However, in 1923 after he had appeared in 216 games for the Ayresome Park club, he was allowed to rejoin Aberdeen. He later had a spell as player-manager of Forress Mechanics and coached the Kent County FA before becoming assistant-manager to Billy Birrell at Chelsea.

DAY, BILLY

Though he was born in Middlesbrough, outside-right Billy Day began his career as an amateur with Sheffield Wednesday. Unable to break into the Owls' first team, he signed professional forms for 'Boro in the summer of 1955 and made his debut the following October in a 4–3 home

win over Leicester City. All of Day's football for Middlesbrough was played in the Second Division but in 1960–61 he broke his leg in a practice game and was forced to miss most of the season. He tried to come back a little too early and his form suffered.

He had scored 21 goals in 131 League and Cup games when he was transferred to Newcastle United for £12,000. He scored on his league debut for the Magpies but it was his only goal in 14 appearances for the St James Park club. Still suffering problems with his leg he moved to Peterborough United before playing non-League football for Cambridge United, then of the Southern League. He had just rediscovered his best form when a bout of pneumonia forced him to retire at the relatively young age of 29.

DEBUTS

Fabrizio Ravanelli scored a hat-trick on his Premiership debut for Middlesbrough on 17 August 1996 who were nevertheless held to a 3–3 draw by Liverpool.

In complete contrast, George Hardwick, who went onto captain both Middlesbrough and England, scored an own goal in the first minute of his debut at home to Bolton Wanderers on 18 December 1937. The Lancashire club went on to win 2–1 with Jack Milsom netting the winner for the Trotters.

DEFEATS - FEWEST

During the 1973–74 season, Middlesbrough went through the 42–match programme and suffered only four defeats as they won the Second Division Championship.

DEFEATS - MOST

A total of 27 defeats suffered during the 1923–24 season is the worst in the club's history. Not surprisingly they finished bottom of the First Division and were relegated.

DEFEATS - WORST

Middlesbrough's record defeat was when Blackburn Rovers beat them 9–0 at Ewood Park on 6 November 1954. The club's worst home defeat is 7–3, a scoreline inflicted upon 'Boro by Bradford City on Christmas Day 1909.

DEFENSIVE RECORD

Middlesbrough's best defensive record over a 42–match Football League

season was established in 1973–74 and helped the club win the Second Division Championship. They conceded just 30 goals in that campaign and were beaten in just four matches.

In 1986–87 the club again conceded just 30 goals, this time from a 46–match programme as they finished runners-up in the Third Division.

Middlesbrough's worst defensive record was in 1953–54 when they conceded 91 goals, finished 21st in the First Division and were relegated.

DELAPENHA, LINDY

Jamaican-born winger Lindy Delapenha had a trial with Arsenal after being demobbed from the RAF but failed to impress and left Highbury to join Portsmouth. His time at Fratton Park coincided with Pompey winning the League Championship in successive seasons and he was restricted to just seven league appearances.

He joined Middlesbrough in April 1950 and made his debut in a 2–1 win at Fulham on the final day of the 1949–50 season. Delapenha missed very few games over the next eight seasons and was the club's leading scorer in 1951–52, 1953–54 and 1955–56. A number of his goals came from the penalty-spot as he gained a reputation as a clinical finisher from the 12–yard mark. He had scored 93 goals in 270 League and Cup games when he was allowed to leave Ayresome Park and join Mansfield Town.

At Field Mill he scored 27 goals in 115 league games before leaving to play non-League football for Burton Albion and later Heanor Town.

DENNISON, BOB

After playing at inside-left for both Newcastle United and Nottingham Forest, Bob Dennison joined Fulham where he was converted into a centre-half. During the Second World War he 'guested' for Northampton Town and after signing for them on a permanent basis, became their manager in 1948.

He left the County Ground in the summer of 1954 to take charge of Middlesbrough. It was Dennison who 'discovered' Brian Clough but in nine years at Ayresome Park he failed to win promotion for the Teeside club even though they came close on a number of occasions. In December 1963 with 19 months of his contract still to run, he was asked to leave. He took 'Boro to the High Court where he won damages of £3,200 for unfair dismissal.

After going into non-League management with Hereford United, he

joined Coventry City as chief scout in December 1967. Following Noel Cantwell's dismissal, Dennison was made caretaker-manager for the last 12 games of the 1971–72 season. When Joe Mercer and Gordon Milne arrived on the scene, he was appointed assistant-manager, though he retained his involvement with the club's scouting system.

DICKS, RONNIE

Utility player Ronnie Dicks played his early football with Dulwich Hamlet before signing amateur forms for Middlesbrough in April 1943. Within a month he had turned professional and appeared in 22 wartime games, mainly as a right-winger. However, when League football resumed after the hostilities, Dicks failed to win a place in the 'Boro side and had to wait until the opening game of the 1947–48 season before making his league debut. He impressed in that game, making both 'Boro goals for Micky Fenton in a 2–2 draw with Manchester United.

Dicks was a first team regular with the Ayresome Park club for 11 seasons and though he appeared in 334 League and Cup games, injuries cost him his place in both the Football League and England 'B' sides.

His younger brother Alan managed Bristol City for 13 years after a playing career with Chelsea, Southend United and Brighton and Hove Albion.

DISMISSALS

The first Middlesbrough player to be dismissed in the Football League was Andy Wilson who was sent-off on 20 March 1915 in a 3–0 home win over Liverpool. However, Jimmy Watson had received his marching orders in the FA Cup match at Preston North End on 16 January 1909.

Bryan Myton was sent-off on his Football League debut on 7 September 1968 as 'Boro lost 2–0 at Cardiff City. Middlesbrough are the only club to have won three Football League away matches in recent years after having had either one player or two sent-off in each instance: v Norwich City (Won 2–0 on 14 August 1968), Aston Villa (Won 2–0 on 27 October 1978), and Crystal Palace (Won 2–1 on 29 December 1979).

DOWNING, DEREK

After having played junior football with his home-town team Doncaster Rovers, Derek Downing left to play non-League football for Frickley Colliery. It was from here that 'Boro manager Raich Carter signed him

in February 1965. After a number of impressive performances for the club's reserve side he made his 'Boro debut in a 1–0 home defeat at the hands of Norwich City in October 1965. Downing went on to appear in 13 league games that season as 'Boro lost their Second Division status. Noted for his very long throw-ins, Downing was an important member of the Middlesbrough side that won promotion at the first attempt in 1966–67. With the exception of the following season when injuries and a loss of form limited his first team appearances, Downing was a regular in the Middlesbrough side for five seasons. During this time he created many of John Hickton's goals with his accurate crosses from the wing but also scored his fair share with 1970–71 being his best season as he netted 13 in 39 games. He took his tally of goals for 'Boro to 48 in 211 League and Cup games before manager Stan Anderson sold him to Orient.

At Brisbane Road he was converted to full-back but having made 100 league appearances he was transferred to York City. He later returned to the north-east to end his career with Hartlepool United.

DRAWS
Middlesbrough played their greatest number of drawn league matches in a single season in 1924–25 when 19 of their matches ended all-square and their fewest the following season when only two of their 42 matches were drawn.

The club's highest scoring draw is 6–6 when they visited Charlton Athletic on 22 October 1960, Brian Clough netting a hat-trick. On 17 October 1936, Middlesbrough drew 5–5 with Sunderland at Ayresome Park with George Camsell scoring a hat-trick. The club have also drawn nine matches 4–4. They were against Bolton Wanderers (Home 1905–06), Blackpool (Home 1926–27), Manchester United (Away 1930–31), Everton (Home 1938–39), Wolves (Home 1948–49), Leeds United (Away 1960–61), Swansea Town (Away 1966–67), Coventry City (Home 1974–75), and Mansfield Town (Home 1985–86) although this latter match was in the League Cup.

E

EARLY GROUNDS

Middlesbrough's first ground was the Archery Ground in Albert Park but in March 1879 the club moved to Breckon Hill Road. Within a year they were on the move again, this time to the Middlesbrough Cricket Club on Linthorpe Road. Here the club built a small main stand with a slate roof and following their acceptance into the Football League, played their first home match in the competition - Small Heath on 9 September 1899 - at the ground.

Even before the club's promotion to the First Division in 1902, they were planning to move to a new ground. After just four months of top flight football the club were told that their lease at Linthorpe Road would not be renewed. The club played its last game at the ground on 25 April 1903, drawing 1–1 with Stoke. Though they only had nine months to build a new ground, Ayresome Park was ready for the start of the 1903–04 season.

ELLIOTT, GEORGE

Sunderland-born George Elliott moved to Middlesbrough when his father, a seafaring captain set up a tugboat company in the town. Though he was a brilliant scholar and his family wanted him to attend Cambridge University, George Elliott loved his football and after playing for Redcar Crusaders and South Bank, he joined Middlesbrough.

His first game for the club was in a 2–0 defeat by Sheffield United

on the opening day of the 1909–10 season. That campaign saw him score four goals in 15 matches, all of them as an inside-forward. Elliott moved to centre-forward midway through the 1912–13 season when his 22 goals in 33 league games made him 'Boro's top scorer for the third successive season. His total included his first hat-trick for the club in a 4–0 home win over Bolton Wanderers.

The following season he not only top-scored for Middlesbrough but his total of 31 goals in 32 games made him the First Division's leading marksman. His total included three hat-tricks against Sunderland (Home 3–4), Blackburn Rovers (Home 3–0), and Sheffield Wednesday (Home 5–2), and this helped him win the first of three full caps for England when he played against Ireland at Ayresome Park.

Elliott who was 'Boro's leading goalscorer in seven league seasons netted five hat-tricks in 1919–20 in wins over Burnley (Home 4–0), Notts County (Home 5–2), Lincoln City (Home 4–1), and Bradford City (Home 4–0 when he scored all four goals), and in a 5–3 defeat at Aston Villa.

Elliott who still holds the club record for the most goals in a single game when he netted 11 for the reserves in a 14–1 win over Houghton Rovers, retired in 1924 despite offers to continue his career with both Newcastle and Sunderland. His total of 213 goals in 365 games, is second only to George Camsell.

EMERSON

Emerson began his career playing for Flamengo, one of Brazil's top club sides but having found his first team opportunities restricted, he moved on to Curitiba. Advised to try his luck in Portugal he joined Belenenses where his performances led to Bobby Robson, then Porto's manager, signing him. In 1996, Emerson was voted Portugal's 'Player of the Year' an award which prompted 'Boro to splash out £4 million on bringing Emerson to the Riverside Stadium.

He made his debut in the 3–3 home draw against Liverpool on the opening day of the 1996–97 season, going on to appear in 32 games. Despite his astute footballing brain and wide range of skills, he was unable to keep 'Boro in the top flight.

Emerson developed a love-hate relationship with the Middlesbrough fans following his well documented absences and at the end of that campaign it was unknown whether he would return to the Riverside to play First Division football. Return he did, taking his tally of goals to 11 in 70 games before one of the most exciting players ever to wear the

colours of Middlesbrough, left the club under a cloud in January 1998 to sign for Tenerife.

EVER-PRESENTS

There have been 42 Middlesbrough players who have been ever-present throughout a Football League season. The greatest number of ever-present seasons by a 'Boro player is seven by David Armstrong. Next in line is goalkeeper Tim Williamson with five.

F

FA CUP

Middlesbrough first entered the FA Cup competition in 1883 and played their first match on 10 November when they entertained Staveley, a Derbyshire mining team. Despite having home advantage, 'Boro were beaten 5–1 with Archie Pringle having the distinction of scoring the club's first FA Cup goal.

In the second round of the 1906–07 FA Cup, Middlesbrough who were members of the First Division were drawn away to Brentford, then members of the Southern League. Middlesbrough had five international players in their team including Steve Bloomer and Alf Common. A record crowd of 21,296 filed into the ground and after ten minutes spilled on to the pitch when fencing collapsed on one side. Brentford scored the only goal of the game after 62 minutes. After the match as the Middlesbrough charabanc wended its way down Brentford High Street, one of the wheels came off!

During the club's Second Division Championship winning season of 1926–27, 'Boro reached the fifth round of the FA Cup for the first time in their history, beating Leicester City (Home 5–3), and Preston North End (Away 3–0) before losing 3–2 at Millwall. The club then proceeded to reach this stage of the competition in three of the next five seasons, before in 1935–36 they won through to the quarter-finals for the first time. That season, 'Boro beat Southampton (Home 1–0), Clapton Orient (Home 3–0), and Leicester City (Home 2–1), before going down 3–1 at Grimsby Town.

When league football resumed in 1946–47, 'Boro again reached the sixth round, beating Queen's Park Rangers (Home 3–1 after a 1–1 draw), Chesterfield (Home 2–1), and Nottingham Forest (Home 6–2 after a 2–2 draw), before losing 1–0 at Burnley after the first meeting at Ayresome Park had ended all-square at 1–1. It was 1969–70 before the club reached the sixth round stage again beating West Ham United (Home 2–1), York City (Home 4–1), and Carlisle United (Away 2–1), before losing to Manchester United 2–1 at Old Trafford after being held to a 1–1 draw at home. From 1974–75, 'Boro made it to the sixth round four times in seven seasons and in the last of these, 1980–81 only went out after extra-time in the replay at Molineux where Wolves won 3–1.

In 1996–97, 'Boro beat Chester City 6–0 in round three but only narrowly defeated non-Leaguers Hednesford Town 3–2. A Juninho goal accounted for Manchester City in the fifth round before the Brazilian and his Italian team-mate Ravanelli scored the goals that gave 'Boro a 2–0 win at Derby County in round six.

Playing in their first-ever FA Cup semi-final, 'Boro went behind to ten men Chesterfield at Old Trafford before goals from Ravanelli and Hignett took the tie into extra-time. Festa put 'Boro ahead only for Chesterfield to grab a sensational equaliser seconds from time. In the replay at Hillsborough, 'Boro made no mistake winning 3–0 with goals from Beck, Ravanelli and Emerson. Just a week after being relegated, 'Boro faced Chelsea in the Wembley final but lost 2–0 after failing to recover from conceding a goal inside 43 seconds!

FA CUP FINAL

Following their relegation from the Premier League, Middlesbrough were looking to rescue their pride in their first-ever FA Cup Final against Chelsea at Wembley. The Italian-inspired Londoners refused to let sentiment stand in their way and with a spectacular long range effort in just 43 seconds, Roberto de Matteo scored the quickest goal in Cup Final history. Eddie Newton killed off 'Boro's fightback with a second goal for Chelsea eight minutes from time in a dreary encounter.

The Middlesbrough team was: Roberts; Blackmore; Fleming; Stamp; Pearson; Festa; Emerson; Mustoe; (Vickers); Ravanelli; (Beck); Juninho; and Hignett; (Kinder).

FATHER AND SON

There have been two instances of fathers and sons playing for

Middlesbrough. The first was Billy and Victor Fox. Billy played for 'Boro in the club's pre-League days and when he hung up his boots remained at Ayresome Park as coach. He held that position when his son Victor, who appeared in 112 games at full-back, scoring his only goal against Blackburn Rovers on his second appearance, was at the club.

The only other father and son to play for 'Boro were Jim Gallagher who made just one appearance for the club before joining Millwall and his son Donald Gallagher who played in 10 wartime games for 'Boro.

FENTON, MICKY

Centre-forward Micky Fenton made a goalscoring debut for Middlesbrough in a 4–0 home win over Blackburn Rovers on the final day of the 1932–33 season. Over the next couple of seasons, Fenton found himself in and out of the Middlesbrough side and it was 1936–37 before he established himself as a first team regular. That season, Fenton was 'Boro's top scorer with 22 goals including his first hat-trick for the club in a 3–2 home win over Manchester United. Fenton headed the scoring charts again in 1937–38, his 24 goals including a hat-trick in the 4–0 home win over Leicester City and all four goals on the final day of the season as West Bromwich Albion were beaten 4–1.

Fenton's best season in terms of goals scored was 1938–39 when his prolific marksmanship earned him a full international cap when he played for England against Scotland. That season, Fenton scored 34 goals in 33 league games, netting hat-tricks in the wins over Huddersfield Town (Home 4–1) and Blackpool (Home 9–2).

During the Second World War, Fenton served with the RAF and played in one unofficial international before returning to Ayresome Park for the resumption of league football in 1946–47. Fenton was more than happy to stay with Middlesbrough despite Everton wanting him as a replacement for Tommy Lawton and responded with 18 goals including four in the 5–4 home defeat of Stoke City. Fenton netted his seventh and final hat-trick for 'Boro the following season when Grimsby Town were beaten 4–1.

Fenton went on to score 162 goals in 269 League and Cup games before becoming the club's coach.

FERNIE, WILLIE

Willie Fernie was playing for Scottish giants Celtic before joining Middlesbrough for a fee of £18,000 in November 1958.

Whilst with the Parkhead club he made 12 appearances at full international level for Scotland including playing in both the 1954 and 1958 World Cup Finals.

He made his 'Boro debut in a 3–2 home defeat by Ipswich Town before going on to play in the remaining 22 games of that 1958–59 season. The following season, the ball-playing inside-forward missed just three games as 'Boro finished the campaign in fifth place in Division Two. A great influence on the younger players at the club, Fernie was allowed to leave Ayresome Park after three games of the 1960–61 season to return to Parkhead. Despite a disappointing return of only three goals in 68 League and Cup games, Fernie certainly created numerous others for the likes of Brian Clough and Alan Peacock. After ending his playing career with Celtic he had a brief spell as manager of Kilmarnock.

FESTA, GIANLUCA

Gianluca Festa played his early football for his home-town team Cagliari and helped them win promotion from Serie 'C' to Serie 'A' in consecutive seasons. His performances led to Inter Milan securing his services and he went on to help them attain success on the domestic front as well as the UEFA Cup.

Middlesbrough paid £2.7 million to bring him to the Riverside Stadium in January 1997 and he made his debut against Sheffield Wednesday where he scored a brilliant goal in a 4–2 win. One of Bryan Robson's most inspired signings, his defensive skills are of the highest quality and though he failed to keep 'Boro in the top flight in his first season on Teeside, he was instrumental in helping them return to the Premiership at the first attempt. In 1997–98 he alternated between full-back and the centre of defence but continued to give wholehearted displays wherever he played. Always enjoying going forward, he scored the club's first goal of the promotion-winning season in a 2–1 win over Charlton Athletic.

The tough-tackling defender has continued to make forages into the opposition penalty area, taking his tally of goals to nine in 126 League and Cup games for the club.

FESTIVAL OF BRITAIN

On 12 May 1951, Middlesbrough entertained Partizan Belgrade of Yugoslavia in the Festival of Britain. 'Boro went down 3–2 with Walker and Mochan scoring their goals in front of an Ayresome Park crowd of 20,000.

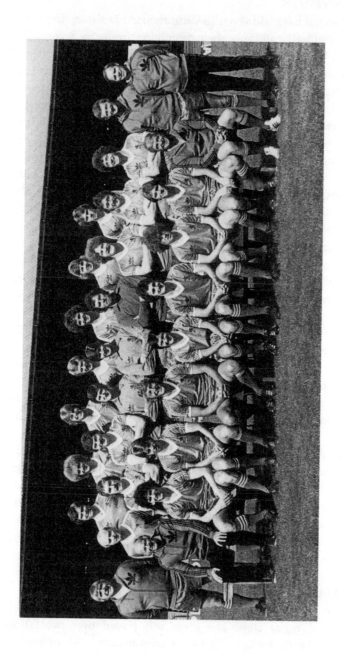

Middlesbrough FC (First Division 1978–79)

FIRST DIVISION

Middlesbrough have had seven spells in the First Division. Their first spell began in 1902–03 following their promotion from the Second Division and lasted 18 seasons. The club's best campaign during this first spell was 1913–14 when they finished third. Following their relegation in 1923–24, 'Boro spent three seasons in Division Two before returning to the top flight. Sadly their second spell in the First Division lasted just one season as they were relegated after finishing bottom with 37 points.

However, 'Boro won the Second Division Championship for a second time in three seasons in 1928–29 to enable them to begin their third spell in Division One. Again the club's stay lasted 18 seasons with their best campaign being 1938–39 when they finished fourth. The club's fourth spell began in 1974–75, following 19 seasons of Second Division football split by just one season of playing in the Third Division.

The club's fourth spell in the First Division lasted eight seasons before they were relegated in 1981–82. Four seasons of Second Division football ended with relegation in 1985–86 before consecutive promotion winning seasons saw 'Boro begin their fifth spell in the First Division in 1988–89.

It lasted just one season before the club won promotion in 1991–92 to the newly formed Premier League. Relegated after one season, 'Boro spent two seasons in the 'new' First Division before returning to Premiership action. Relegated in 1996–97, 'Boro finished the following campaign as runners-up to Nottingham Forest to end their seventh spell of First Division football with promotion to the Premier League.

FIRST LEAGUE MATCH

Middlesbrough's first Football League match saw them travel to Lincoln City on 2 September 1899 in a Second Division match. Despite having a good number of opportunities to score, 'Boro lost 3–0. The Middlesbrough side was: E.Smith; T.Shaw; A.Ramsey; H.Allport; J.McNally; J.McCracken; R.Wanlass; G.Longstaffe; J.Gettins; R.Page and C.Pugh.

FIRST MATCH

The club's first-ever match was played in 1877 against Tees Wanderers, a leading local rugby club. The game was played over two 20 minute halves and the final score was 1–1. Unfortunately it is not known who the Middlesbrough goalscorer was.

FITZSIMONS, ARTHUR

Middlesbrough manager David Jack paid Irish club Shelbourne £18,000 for the services of Arthur Fitzsimons in May 1949. Despite not having made his first team debut he was capped at full international level four months later when he played for the Republic of Ireland side against Finland in a World Cup qualifying game.

In fact, Fitzsimons had to wait until April 1950 before making his league debut for 'Boro in a 3–0 win at West Bromwich Albion. His first three seasons at Ayresome Park saw him appear in just 25 league games but after winning a regular place in the side at the start of the 1952–53 season he went on to appear in 231 games for the club. Fitzsimons scored 51 goals with a best return of 14 in 1955–56.

On leaving 'Boro he had a short spell with Lincoln City where he made another international appearance to add to the 25 he had made whilst with Middlesbrough. He later played for Mansfield Town where he ended his league career.

FJORTOFT, JAN AAGE

Norwegian international Jan Aage Fjortoft began his Football League career with Swindon Town who paid £500,000 for the striker from Rapid Vienna in July 1993.

He had scored 39 goals in 85 games for Swindon when Middlesbrough paid a record £1.3 million for him in March 1995. He made his debut in a 3–1 win at West Bromwich Albion, going on to score three goals in eight games as 'Boro clinched the First Division Championship. Though over the next couple of seasons, goals were hard to come by, his value to the team was more than just putting the ball into the net. Able to shield the ball from defenders, his deft touches and enthusiasm made him a great favourite with the Middlesbrough crowd. He went on to score 13 goals in 50 games for 'Boro before Sheffield United paid £700,000 in January 1997 to take him to Bramall Lane.

After a quiet debut for the Blades against his old club, Swindon Town, he scored eight goals in eight games including a hat-trick in a 3–1 win over Grimsby Town. He almost returned to the Premier League in his first season with United but they were beaten in the dying seconds of the play-off final against Crystal Palace. Despite scoring 12 goals in 18 starts including another hat-trick in a 5–1 win over Stockport County, he couldn't hold down a regular place and in January 1998 joined Barnsley for £800,000.

Despite failing to save the club from relegation from the Premier League, Fjortoft, who scored six goals in 15 games always looked likely to give the fans something to cheer about. He had scored 13 goals in 40 games for the Oakwell club when in November 1998 he was transferred to Eintrackt Frankfurt for £450,000.

FLEMING, CURTIS
Full-back Curtis Fleming joined Middlesbrough from Irish part-timers St Patrick's Athletic in the summer of 1991 for a fee of £50,000 and made his debut as a substitute for Gary Parkinson in a 2–1 home defeat by Ipswich Town in the third game of the 1991–92 season. After replacing Parkinson on a permanent basis, Fleming faced stiff opposition to hold on to his place, first from Chris Morris who joined the club from Celtic and Neil Cox who joined 'Boro from Aston Villa. Fleming withstood the challenges and showed his versatility by being able to play on either flank.

Renowned for his strong tackling, Fleming overcame a career threatening injury to win the first of 10 caps for the Republic of Ireland as a substitute for Denis Irwin against Czechoslovakia in April 1996. That month also saw Fleming score his first league goal for the club in a 2–1 home defeat by Wimbledon. Fleming enjoyed his best season in the top flight in 1996–97, being outstanding in both of the club's cup runs and their unsuccessful bid to retain Premier League status.

One of Middlesbrough's most consistent performers, his first team appearances in recent seasons have been reduced by a series of niggling injuries but nonetheless, the Manchester-born defender has played in 271 games for the Riverside club.

FLOODLIGHTS
The first floodlight game at Ayresome Park was a friendly match against Sunderland on 16 October 1957. 'Boro watched by a crowd of 27,273 won 2–0 with goals from Fitzsimons and Clough. The cost of installing the floodlights was £18,000.

FOGGON, ALAN
An England Youth international, Alan Foggon came through the junior ranks with Newcastle United and when he made the first team, he became part of the Magpies' side that won the Fairs Cup in 1969. In fact, Foggon scored one of the goals in the second leg of the final against Ujpest Dozsa. After netting 16 goals in 80 games for Newcastle,

he left St James Park to join Cardiff City for £25,000.

His stay at Ninian Park was short-lived as he did little to impress Jimmy Scoular who accused him of being consistently overweight. Therefore, it came as no surprise when he returned to the north-east in October 1972, joining Middlesbrough for £10,000.

Foggon's arrival at Ayresome Park coincided with him being midway through a three-week suspension and he had to wait until the end of November before making his debut in a 2–0 defeat at home to Swindon Town. When 'Boro won the Second Division Championship in 1973–74, Foggon was the club's leading scorer with 19 goals in 41 games.

He continued to find the net the following season, topping the club's scoring charts with 16 goals as they finished seventh in Division One. Foggon went on to score 49 goals in 136 games for 'Boro before joining Manchester United for £27,000. After just three appearances as a substitute for the Old Trafford club, he played for Sunderland, Southend and Hartlepool before going into non-League football with Consett.

FOOTBALL LEAGUE CUP

Middlesbrough's first match in the Football League Cup saw them go down 4–3 at home to Cardiff City on 3 October 1960 in front of an Ayresome Park crowd of 15,695. The following season Alan Peacock scored the club's first hat-trick in the competition in a 6–3 win at Tranmere Rovers but after beating Crewe Alexandra in the second round, 'Boro lost 3–2 at Norwich City. In 1962–63, Middlesbrough were drawn against Hull City but in a tie that required three games, 'Boro again went out at the first hurdle. In fact, it was 1974–75 before the club made any impression on the competition when after beating Tottenham Hotspur (Away 4–0), Leicester City (Home 1–0), and Liverpool (Away 1–0), they lost 3–0 at Old Trafford against a Manchester United side who had been fortunate to escape from the first meeting at Ayresome Park with a goalless draw.

The following season 'Boro went one better and reached the League Cup semi-final for the first time. Wins over Bury (Away 2–1), Derby County (Home 1–0), Peterborough United (Home 3–0), and Burnley (Away 2–0), brought them face to face with Manchester City in the two-legged semi-final. A David Armstrong goal gave 'Boro a 1–0 win in the first leg at Ayresome Park but the Teeside club crashed 4–0 in the second leg at Maine Road.

Middlesbrough reached the semi-final stage for a second time in

1991–92 when after defeating Third Division Bournemouth 3–2 on aggregate, they beat Barnsley (Home 1–0), Manchester City (Home 2–1), and Peterborough United (Home 1–0 after a goalless draw). Their opponents were Manchester United who once again were lucky to come away from the first leg at Ayresome Park unscathed, the game ending goalless. At Old Trafford in the second leg, Bernie Slaven scored for Middlesbrough but United won 2–1 after extra-time.

In 1996–97, Hereford United were on the receiving end of four Ravanelli goals as 'Boro triumphed 7–0 in the first leg at the Riverside. A 3–0 win in the return at Edgar Street gave the club their biggest-ever aggregate win, 10–0. Huddersfield Town were also well beaten in the third round, 5–1 before 'Boro produced two of their most passionate League Cup displays to beat Newcastle United (Home 3–1) and Liverpool (Home 2–1). In the semi-final, 'Boro faced giant-killers Stockport County, winning the first leg at Edgeley Park 2–0. However, they had a scare in the return at the Riverside, going down 1–0 to a side that almost snatched an equaliser. The final against Leicester City was disappointing but when Ravanelli put 'Boro ahead in extra-time it looked as if the trophy was going to the north-east. Leicester though grabbed a late equaliser and then won 1–0 in the replay at Hillsborough.

'Boro enjoyed success in the League Cup for a second successive season in 1997–98. After beating Barnet 3–0 on aggregate, Middlesbrough defeated Sunderland 2–0 at the Riverside with goals from Campbell and Hignett. Extra-time was required to beat fourth round opponents Bolton Wanderers 2–1 and after a Craig Hignett goal had accounted for Reading, 'Boro met Liverpool in the semi-final. In the first leg at Anfield, 'Boro lost 2–1 but with Merson and Branca scoring inside the first four minutes of the return, 'Boro won 3–2 on aggregate to win through to the final for the second year in succession. With the exception of 'keeper Mark Schwarzer, 'Boro were below par and lost 2–0 after extra-time to Chelsea, on a day when Paul Gascoigne found his way into the referee's notebook on his return to English football.

FORMATION

It was once thought that Middlesbrough Football Club was founded at a tripe supper at the Corporation Hotel but it has been discovered that members of Middlesbrough Cricket Club were in fact responsible for forming it at a meeting in the gymnasium of the Albert Park Hotel in 1875.

Middlesbrough first turned professional in 1889, then reverted to amateur status in 1892 and finally decided on permanent professional ranking in 1899 though the club had already won the FA Amateur Cup in 1895 and 1898.

FORREST, BILLY

A Scottish Schoolboy international, Billy Forrest had played his early football for Musselburgh juniors before joining Edinburgh St Bernards where his impressive performances made him the target of a number of top clubs. It was Middlesbrough manager Peter McWilliam who secured Forrest's signature and the youngster made his 'Boro debut in a 3–0 win at Manchester United in January 1930. After appearing in 10 league games that season, Forrest won a regular place in the 'Boro side at the start of the following campaign, going on to score eight goals from his position at left-half in 333 League and Cup games.

During the war years he appeared in a further 128 games for the club before retiring in 1945. He remained at Ayresome Park until late 1946 coaching the club's juniors but then took up an appointment as manager of Darlington. The Quakers had record crowds after a good start to the 1948–49 season, eventually finishing fourth in the Third Division (North). Forrest later ran a hotel in Billington but in 1956 was partially paralysed after an accident, which led to his death.

FREEMAN, REG

Full-back Reg Freeman began his career with Northern Nomads but in 1920 he joined Oldham Athletic where he was appointed club captain for the 1922–23 season. His displays for the Latics led to him being named as reserve for the Football League XI to play the League of Ireland and selection for an England trial game.

In May 1923, Middlesbrough paid the Boundary Park club £3,600 for Freeman's services and he made his debut in a 1–0 defeat at Huddersfield Town on the opening day of the 1923–24 season. Despite a series of injuries that reduced his appearances in 1927–28 to just four, Freeman was a regular in the Middlesbrough side for seven seasons. He won two Second Division Championship medals in 1926–27 and 1928–29 but at the end of the following season, Freeman who had played in 187 games left Ayresome Park to join Rotherham United for £150.

He was to give the Millmoor club 22 years service as a player and a manager. When playing left-back for the club's reserve side against

Wombwell in December 1931 he scored a second-half hat-trick that included two penalties. In January 1934 he became player-manager and in the years leading up to the Second World War he brought about a consistency not seen before at Millmoor. In 1950–51 he led the Millers to promotion, eventually reaping the rewards for all his hard work. In August 1952 he left to manage Sheffield United and at the end of his first season in charge they won the Second Division Championship. Sadly, Reg Freeman died while still in office in August 1955.

FREIGHT ROVER TROPHY

A competition designed solely and specifically for the Associate Members of the Football League, the Freight Rover Trophy replaced the initial Associate Members Cup for the 1984–85 season.

Middlesbrough first participated in 1986–87 and despite mixed results in the preliminary group matches - Doncaster Rovers (Home 3–0), and Chesterfield (Away 1–2) they still qualified for the knockout stages. Goals from Kernaghan and Ripley gave 'Boro a 2–1 first round win at Halifax Town. In round two, 'Boro played out a goalless draw against Rochdale at Spotland before winning 4–3 on penalties. 'Boro were now in the area semi-final but went out of the competition when they lost 1–0 at home to Mansfield Town.

FULL MEMBERS' CUP

Called the Full Members' Cup because it was originally open only to First and Second Division clubs, 'Boro entered the competition in 1985–86. Following a 2–0 home win over Carlisle United, 'Boro met Hull City in the Northern Area semi-final. Bernie Slaven opened the scoring for 'Boro but by the end of ninety minutes, the Tigers had levelled the scores. Despite applying a lot of pressure in extra-time it was Hull City who won through to the Northern Area final with a 3–1 victory.

G

GASCOIGNE, PAUL

First associated with Newcastle United as a schoolboy, Paul Gascoigne progressed through the ranks to make his league debut a month before turning professional. Quickly establishing himself as the most exciting talent of his generation, he was voted Young Player of the Year by the PFA in 1988. His sense of humour occasionally got him into trouble but in the summer of 1988 after he had scored 25 goals in 107 games for the Magpies, Spurs manager Terry Venables signed Gazza for a British record fee of £2 million, knowing that he could harness Gascoigne's talents without removing the impishness that delighted the British public. Within 11 days of his Spurs debut at Newcastle, where the Geordie fans pelted him with Mars bars, he won his first full England cap playing as a substitute against Denmark. He was immediately hailed as the player around whom England should build its team for the 1990 World Cup. He was the undoubted star in England's march to the semi-finals. His televised tears when he realised a booking in the semi-final would rule him out of the final should England progress, endeared him to the nation, who in turn voted him BBC Television Sports Personality of the Year. He continued where he left off in 1990–91, steering Spurs almost single-handedly to the FA Cup Final. His day was ruined after only 15 minutes by a serious ligament injury caused by a rash challenge on his part and he was carried off. The career threatening damage to his cruciate ligament put his record £8.5 million move to Lazio in jeopardy but

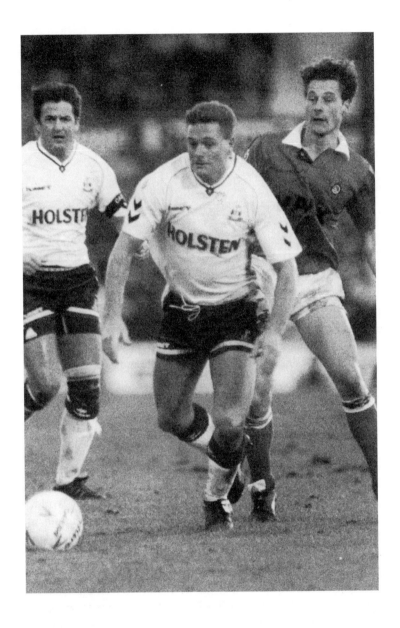

Paul Gascoigne

after taking a year to recover, he eventually moved for £5.5 million to show the Italians what he could do, having scored 33 goals in 113 games for the White Hart Lane club.

In the summer of 1995 he joined Glasgow Rangers for £4.3 million and in his first season at Ibrox, helped the club win the Scottish Premier Division Championship and the Scottish Cup. In 1996–97 he won another Premier Division Championship and helped Rangers lift the Scottish League Cup. He had scored 39 goals in 105 games for Rangers when Middlesbrough paid £3.45 million for his services on transfer deadline day in March 1998.

Gascoigne became the first player to make his debut in a Wembley Cup Final when he came off the bench in the 63rd minute in the 2–0 League Cup Final defeat by Chelsea. There is little doubt that his charisma both on and off the field contributed to 'Boro's late successful surge for automatic promotion to the Premiership. Sadly though he was not a member of England's World Cup squad in France '98 following a well documented argument with England manager Glenn Hoddle.

In 1998–99, Gascoigne who has won 57 caps for England, demonstrated that he had lost none of his abundant skills, working extremely hard for the cause of Middlesbrough Football Club, and by the end of the 1999-2000 season, despite an injury-troubled campaign, had scored four goals in 48 games for the north-east side.

GATES, BILL

The captain of the England Youth team, Bill Gates joined Middlesbrough as an amateur and made his first team debut at the age of 17 years 142 days old in a 3–2 defeat at Luton Town in September 1961. Gates was to remain at Ayresome Park for 13 seasons yet in that time he was never considered an automatic choice. His best campaign was 1970–71 when he appeared in 39 games as 'Boro finished seventh in Division Two. He helped the club win promotion to the Second Division in 1966–67, his only goal that campaign helping 'Boro beat Scunthorpe United 2–1.

One of the club's bravest players, he once fractured his jaw in a League Cup match against Manchester United but showed his bravery by playing on, although 'Boro lost 1–0. Gates went on to score 12 goals in 329 games for the club but only made two appearances in the club's promotion-winning season of 1973–74. At the end of that campaign he was awarded a testimonial against League Champions Leeds United.

On retirement he went into the sports retail business and after selling up, became a wealthy man, and now lives in the Cayman Islands.

GILLOW, WILF

Preston-born Wilf Gillow played non-League football for Lancaster Town and Fleetwood before joining Blackpool in 1912. He made 27 appearances for the Seasiders before signing for his home-town club. He played for North End either side of the First World War before leaving to join Grimsby Town.

He later became player-manager of the Blundell Park club and in 1928–29 led the Mariners to promotion to the First Division. However, after just two seasons in the top flight, Grimsby were relegated and in April 1932, he resigned his post. He was out of the game until March 1934 when he replaced Peter McWilliam as Middlesbrough's manager.

In his first season with the club, 'Boro just avoided relegation but after that, improved their league placing with each campaign. In 1938–39 'Boro finished fourth in Division One and it seemed only a matter of time before they won the League Championship but sadly the Second World War ended their title hopes. Gillow remained as 'Boro boss on a part-time basis as the club played regional league football. He died whilst in office following complications after an operation.

GOALKEEPERS

Middlesbrough FC has almost always been extremely well served by its goalkeepers and most of them have been highly popular with the supporters.

One of the club's earliest 'keepers was Jeremiah Dawkins who played for 'Boro in the 1880s. On one occasion against Ecclesfield, he decided to help out his forwards and raced upfield to join in the attack. His opposite number thwarted the move and noticed that he was out of his goal. He kicked the ball out to his unmarked outside-left who tapped the ball into the empty goal!

Tim Williamson made his Middlesbrough debut against Bristol City in April 1902 and was the club's first-choice 'keeper for the next 20 years. He played in 602 League and Cup games, a club record that still stands today. An England international, he went on to win seven caps despite putting through his own goal on his debut against Ireland at Ayresome Park.

Jimmy Mathieson joined 'Boro from Raith Rovers in June 1926 and

missed just two games in his first three seasons with the club as they experienced promotion, relegation and promotion in successive seasons. He went on to appear in 264 games before leaving to join Brentford.

Dave Cumming was another Scottish goalkeeper who arrived at the club from Arbroath in October 1936 for a fee of £3,000, making him the most expensive 'keeper to come south of the border. Whilst with 'Boro he won full international honours for Scotland but after appearing in 157 games, he dislocated a kneecap in the match against Blackpool in April 1947 and had to retire.

Italian-born Rolando Ugolini moved to Scotland with his family and after impressing in junior football, joined Celtic. After refusing a move to Chelsea, he joined Middlesbrough and though he conceded seven goals on his first appearance in a pre-season practice game, he went on to be the club's regular 'keeper for nine seasons, appearing in 335 games.

Over the next few seasons, Peter Taylor who was perhaps better known as Brian Clough's managerial partner was the club's custodian. Signed from Coventry City, he played in 146 games before leaving to play for Port Vale. Willie Whigham arrived at Ayresome Park from Falkirk and in his first season with the club helped them win promotion to the Second Division. Though he was often erratic, Whigham played in 210 games for 'Boro before giving way to Jim Platt.

One of the best post-war goalkeepers to come from the Emerald Isle, Platt cost 'Boro £7,000 when he arrived at Ayresome Park from Ballymena in the summer of 1970. Platt, who won 20 full caps for Northern Ireland went on to play in 481 games during 12 seasons with 'Boro.

Unable to win a regular place in the Manchester United side, Stephen Pears joined Middlesbrough, the club he had trials with prior to going to Old Trafford. He was 'Boro's first-choice 'keeper for 10 seasons, appearing in 424 games and was without doubt one of the best goalkeepers never to have played for England.

The club's present goalkeeper is Australian international Mark Schwarzer who joined the club from Bradford City in February 1997 for £1.5 million and has played in 132 games.

GOALS

The most goals Middlesbrough have scored in one match came in their 11–0 victory over Scarborough in a qualifying round of the FA Cup competition of 1890–91. In the Football League, 'Boro's biggest win is the 9–0 victory over Brighton and Hove Albion on 23 August 1958.

GOALS - CAREER BEST

The highest goalscorer in the club's history is George Camsell who, between seasons 1925–26 and 1938–39, netted 345 goals for the club. These comprised 325 in the League and 20 in the FA Cup.

GOALS - INDIVIDUAL

Four players have scored five goals in a game for Middlesbrough. The first was Andy Wilson who netted all five goals in 'Boro's 5–2 win over Nottingham Forest on 6 October 1923. On Christmas Day 1926, George Camsell scored all five goals as 'Boro won 5–3 at Manchester City. Camsell repeated the feat on 9 September 1935 as 'Boro beat Aston Villa at Villa Park 7–2. The last player to achieve the feat was Brian Clough who, on 22 August 1958, scored five of Middlesbrough's goals in a 9–0 home win over Brighton and Hove Albion.

GOALS - SEASON

The club's highest league goalscorer in any one season remains George Camsell who scored a remarkable 59 league goals as Middlesbrough won the Second Division Championship in 1926–27. He also scored four goals in the FA Cup to take his season's tally to 63. In the league he scored all five goals in a 5–3 win at Manchester City, four in the matches against Portsmouth (Home 7–3), Fulham (Home 6–1), and Swansea Town (Home 7–1), and hat-tricks against Notts County (Home 4–2), Port Vale (Home 5–1), Grimsby Town (Away 7–4), South Shields (Home 5–0), and Reading (Home 5–0). He also netted a hat-trick in a 3–0 FA Cup win over Preston North End.

GORDON, JIMMY

Tough-tackling right-half Jimmy Gordon began his Football League career with Newcastle United. He had made 132 league appearances for the Magpies before his transfer to Middlesbrough at the end of the Second World War. He played in 21 games during the 1945–46 season and in six games of the club's FA Cup run to the fifth round.

He made his league debut for 'Boro in a 1–0 win at Aston Villa on the opening day of the 1946–47 season and went on to be a first team regular for the next six seasons. He played the last of his 253 League and Cup games in a 2–2 draw at Sheffield United in February 1954.

During the early part of the 1960s, Gordon returned to Ayresome Park to take charge of the club's junior side before becoming reserve team

trainer to Blackburn Rovers. He was later trainer to Derby County when they won the League Championship in 1971–72 and teamed up with Brian Clough and Peter Taylor again when they were in charge of Nottingham Forest and shared in the City Ground club's European success.

GRIFFITHS, TOM

A tall centre-half, Tom Griffiths began his career with Wrexham and succeeded the immortal Fred Keenor as the regular Welsh centre-half. In 1927 he moved to Everton but in 1929–30 he was a member of the side that suffered the indignity of being relegated for the first time in the club's history. He played for the first half of the following season but after losing his place to Charlie Gee, he left to play for Bolton Wanderers. After the Lancashire club lost their top flight status, Griffiths joined Middlesbrough and made his debut in a 2–2 home draw against Birmingham. Griffiths who won 21 caps for Wales, spent four seasons at Ayresome Park and appeared in 92 League and Cup games. His only goal for 'Boro came in a 2–2 draw at Derby County in April 1933 to earn the club a valuable point in their fight against relegation. One of the club's best-ever defenders, he left to play for Aston Villa in November 1935 but despite his heroic efforts, the Midlands club was still relegated. On leaving Villa Park he became Wrexham's player-coach, later being appointed director of the Racecourse Ground club.

GUEST PLAYERS

The 'guest' system was used by all clubs during the two wars. Although at times it was abused almost beyond belief (in that some sides that opposed Middlesbrough had ten or 11 'guests'!) it normally worked sensibly and effectively to the benefit of players, clubs and supporters alike.

The most distinguished players to 'guest' for 'Boro were Matt Busby (Liverpool), Wilf Copping (Leeds United), Johnny Carey (Manchester United), and Bill Nicholson (Tottenham Hotspur).

H

HAMILTON, GARY

Glasgow-born winger Gary Hamilton first came to Middlesbrough for a one day trial following a recommendation from the club's Scottish scout. He was later invited back for a lengthier trial period after which he joined the club as an apprentice.

He made his 'Boro debut in a 3–1 defeat at Bolton Wanderers in February 1983 whilst still an apprentice, signing professional forms three months later. The following season he won international recognition when he was selected for the Scotland Youth side to play Russia. Following 'Boro's relegation to the Third Division in 1985–86, Hamilton was offered the chance to join Charlton Athletic but turned down the opportunity, preferring to fight it out with Middlesbrough.

He continued to be an important member of the 'Boro side and helped them win promotion from the Third Division in 1986–87 and to the top flight via the play-offs the following season.

In 1988–89, Hamilton suffered with a series of injuries and at the end of the season he was forced to retire, aged just 24. Hamilton, who had scored 29 goals in 272 games for 'Boro was awarded a testimonial match against Sunderland after which he became a coach in Texas.

HARDWICK, GEORGE

One of Middlesbrough's best known players, George Hardwick made his first team debut in December 1937, scoring an own goal inside the first

minute in a 2–1 home defeat at the hands of Bolton Wanderers. He made eight appearances that season but spent the entire 1938–39 campaign in the reserves.

During the Second World War, Hardwick served in the RAF Bomber Command. He also 'guested' for Chelsea and appeared in two wartime Wembley Cup Finals for the Stamford Bridge club. Hardwick was selected for 17 wartime internationals, all as captain.

When League football resumed in 1946–47, Hardwick was in 'Boro's starting line-up for the first game against Aston Villa which they won 1–0 through a Wilf Mannion goal. He was a virtual ever-present for the next five seasons during which time his consistency in the 'Boro defence earned him 13 full caps for England.

His first full international appearance came against Scotland at Wembley in April 1947 when he captained England in a 1–1 draw. In fact, Hardwick captained his country in each of his international appearances and the Great Britain side which played against Europe.

Hardwick left Ayresome Park in November 1950 after scoring seven goals in 166 games to become player-manager of Oldham Athletic.

Hardwick exerted a great influence on the Boundary Park club and in 1952–53, the Latics won the Third Division (North) Championship. However, a lack of finance precluded any significant strengthening of the side and the following season the club were relegated after just one campaign of Second Division football. Hardwick resigned his post in 1956 with the Latics still struggling.

Following spells coaching the US Army, PSV Eindhoven and the Dutch FA, Hardwick returned to Ayresome Park in 1961 as the club's Youth team coach. In November 1964 he joined Sunderland as manager but in spite of leading the Wearsiders to their highest post-war league position, he was dismissed. He later managed Gateshead and in 1983, he and Wilf Mannion were given a joint testimonial by Middlesbrough. George Hardwick is a regular visitor to the club's Riverside Stadium where he has a suite named after him.

HARRIS, BILL

Bill Harris began his career with his home-town club, Swansea but having failed to make the grade was released following his National Service. After a short spell with Llanelli, he joined Hull City who were more than happy to pay out £2,000 for his services. Harris stayed at Boothferry Park for four seasons, appearing in 145 games for the Tigers

before his move to Middlesbrough for £15,000 in March 1954.

Harris' first game for 'Boro was in a 3–3 home draw against Chelsea and though he played in nine of the remaining ten games that season, he couldn't prevent the club being relegated to Division Two.

It wasn't long before Harris was converted from wing-half to inside-forward and with great success. He stayed at Ayresome Park for 11 seasons, being ever-present in 1955–56 and 1956–57. His performances for 'Boro led to him winning six full caps for Wales, the first against Austria just a couple of months after joining the Teeside club. Harris went on to score 72 goals in 378 games with a best of 14 in 1961–62, a total which included a hat-trick in a 4–3 win at Newcastle United.

On leaving Middlesbrough, he joined Bradford City as player-manager but after just one unsuccessful season at Valley Parade he returned to Teeside to manage Stockton.

HAT-TRICKS

The scorer of the club's first hat-trick in the Football League was Joe Murphy in the 8–1 home win over Burton Swifts on 11 November 1899.

George Camsell scored a record nine hat-tricks during the club's Second Division Championship-winning season of 1926–27 in his record total of 59 goals.

In the 1958–59 season, Brian Clough scored hat-tricks against the same side in both the home and away matches on two occasions. He netted hat-tricks in the matches against Brighton and Hove Albion (Home 9–0 and Away 6–4) and Scunthorpe United (Home 6–1 and Away 3–0). Fabrizio Ravanelli scored a hat-trick on his debut for the club in a 3–3 draw at home to Liverpool on the opening day of the 1996–97 season.

HENDRIE, JOHN

A Scottish Youth international, he began his career with Coventry City but in three seasons at Highfield Road, he only played in 23 games. Following a loan spell with Hereford United, he joined Bradford City on a free transfer. In his first season at Valley Parade, Hendrie helped the Bantams win promotion to the Second Division. He stayed with Bradford City for four years, scoring 59 goals in 215 games before Newcastle manager Willie McFaul paid £500,000 for his services in the summer of 1988.

In his only season at St James Park, the Magpies were relegated and Hendrie moved on in the close season to join Leeds United. Again he only stayed for one season but this time the campaign was more successful as the Elland Road club won the Second Division Championship and promotion to the top flight.

In July 1990, 'Boro manager Colin Todd splashed out £550,000 to bring Hendrie to Ayresome Park and he made his debut in a goalless draw at home to West Ham United on the opening day of the 1990–91 season. The following season he helped the club win promotion to the newly-formed Premier League and though 'Boro were relegated after just one season in the top flight, Hendrie had a successful season, scoring nine goals in 32 games including a hat-trick in a 3–2 home win over Blackburn Rovers. Playing in a more central striking role, Hendrie continued to find the net the following season, scoring his second hat-trick for the club in the final game of the campaign, a 5–2 win at Charlton Athletic. When 'Boro won the First Division Championship in 1994–95, Hendrie was the club's leading scorer with 15 goals, including a hat-trick

John Hendrie

in a 3–0 win at Burnley. Injuries hampered his last season with the club and in October 1996 after scoring 55 goals in 234 games he moved to Barnsley for a fee of £250,000.

The veteran striker became the club's player-manager following the departure of Danny Wilson to Sheffield Wednesday but has since reverted to concentrating on playing after Dave Bassett became the Oakwell manager in the summer of 1999.

HICKTON, JOHN

John Hickton began his league career with Sheffield Wednesday whom he joined straight from school and made his debut at left-back in the match against Aston Villa in March 1964. He had once scored eight goals from the centre-forward position in an FA Youth Cup game and it was to this position he reverted when playing for the Owls' Central League side. His prolific goalscoring feats for Wednesday's reserve side led to the club giving him another chance. He responded by scoring 21 goals in 52 games including a hat-trick in a 4–0 win over Arsenal, but in September 1966 he was rather surprisingly allowed to join Middlesbrough for £20,000.

He scored from the penalty-spot on his 'Boro debut in a 3–2 home win over Workington and ended the season in which the club won promotion to the Second Division with 15 goals in 40 games including a hat-trick in a 4–0 defeat of Torquay United. In 1967–68, Hickton topped the club's scoring charts for the first of six occasions, netting another hat-trick in a 5–0 home win over Plymouth Argyle in his total of 29 goals.

The following season he scored four goals in the 5–3 win over Hull City, whilst other hat-tricks followed against Queen's Park Rangers (Home 6–2 in 1970–71) and Orient (Home 3–2 in 1972–73). Hickton went on to score 185 goals in 482 League and Cup games before following a loan spell with Hull City, he went to play for Fort Lauderdale in the NASL. After recovering from breaking his leg whilst playing in the States he returned to England to play non-League football for Whitby Town.

HIGNETT, CRAIG

Craig Hignett began is Football League career with Crewe Alexandra after being released by Liverpool. A prolific goalscorer in his days at Gresty Road, he had netted 57 times in 150 League and Cup games

before Middlesbrough paid £500,000 to bring the speedy winger to Teeside in November 1992.

His first game for 'Boro was in a 4–1 defeat at Oldham Athletic as the club went on to be relegated at the end of that campaign. The following season he scored four goals in a 5–0 League Cup win over Brighton and Hove Albion and in 1994–95 helped 'Boro win the First Division Championship. He made a good start to the 1995–96 season, scoring seven goals in the first 16 games being preferred to John Hendrie. Just when he seemed to be forming a good strike partnership with Nick Barmby, he was sidelined by a knee injury.

Desperate to be retained, he asked for a cut in salary and in 1996–97 proved to be one of 'Boro's unsung heroes as they reached the finals of both the FA and League Cups. His workrate was top-class and his cool finishing led to him scoring seven goals, two from the penalty-spot. After finding himself out of contract at Middlesbrough, he spent a few months at Aberdeen after joining the Dons on a free transfer. In November 1998, Barnsley paid £800,000 to take him to Oakwell. An instant hit with the Barnsley fans he has scored a goal every other game for the Tykes including one in the 1999-2000 Division One play-off final.

HODGSON, DAVID

Gateshead-born striker David Hodgson had trials with Ipswich, Bolton and Sheffield Wednesday before signing for Middlesbrough. After progressing through the ranks he made his first team debut as a substitute for Tony McAndrew in a 2–2 draw at Nottingham Forest in September 1978. It was later that campaign that he established himself in the Middlesbrough side and over the next four seasons he went on to give the club great service. Though he made numerous chances for his fellow strikers, Hodgson did net one hat-trick in Middlesbrough colours as they beat Spurs 4–1 in December 1980. His performances led to him winning international recognition for England at Under-23 level, but in August 1982 after scoring 20 goals in 140 games he left Ayresome Park to join Liverpool for £450,000.

Although much was expected of him at Anfield, he proved to be a disappointment. After just 21 appearances and four goals, he was sold to Sunderland for the knockdown price of £125,000. Whilst with the Wearsiders he played in the 1985 League Cup Final against his next club, Norwich City.

He returned to Middlesbrough on loan early in 1987 but was sent-off

against Bristol City in only his second game and returned to Carrow Road. Towards the end of his playing career he turned out for both Swansea and Sheffield Wednesday and had spells with Spanish club Jerez, Metz of France and Mazda in Japan before becoming manager of Darlington whom he took to the play-off final in 1999-2000.

David Hodgson

HOLLIDAY, EDDIE

Outside-left Eddie Holliday made his Middlesbrough debut in a 2–1 defeat at West Ham United in December 1957, going on to play in all the remaining 22 games of the season as 'Boro finished seventh in Division Two. An important member of the Middlesbrough attack, his pin-point crosses provided Clough and Peacock with numerous chances, most of which they tucked away. After two seasons in the club's first team, he won international recognition when he was elected for England at Under-23 level. A month later, in October 1959, Holliday made his full international debut alongside Brian Clough in a 1–1 draw against Wales at Ninian Park. He won two further caps with 'Boro before leaving Ayresome Park in March 1962 to join Sheffield Wednesday.

He never really settled at Hillsborough and after just 55 league appearances for the Owls he rejoined Middlesbrough. He took his tally of goals in his two spells with the club to 25 in 169 games but following their relegation to the Third Division at the end of his first season back, he left to play Southern League football for Hereford United.

In February 1968 he returned to league football with Workington but after making 56 appearances, left to play for Peterborough United. He had made 16 league appearances for 'Posh' when he broke his leg and had to retire.

HOLMES, WALTER

After training to become a school-teacher at Bede College, where playing at outside-right he established a record of 38 goals, he played non-League football for Willington Athletic. After helping them win the Northern League Championship in 1913–14, he left to sign professional forms for 'Boro, though the Ayresome Park club allowed him to continue to work as a teacher.

Having been converted to full-back, he made his first team debut for Middlesbrough in a 1–0 home win over Manchester City in February 1915. He appeared in 10 league games at the end of that season before seeing active service in France during the First World War. Despite contracting bronchial pneumonia, he had recovered sufficiently to take his place in the 'Boro side when League football resumed in 1919–20.

He went on to appear in 174 games for the Ayresome Park club before being given a free transfer and joining Darlington. He played for one season with the Quakers before hanging up his boots. A teetotaller and a Methodist lay preacher, Walter 'Squire' Holmes as he was known became a headmaster.

HOME MATCHES

Middlesbrough's best home win is the 10–3 defeat of Sheffield United in a First Division match on 18 November 1933. The club have also scored nine goals at home on four occasions - Gainsborough Trinity (9–2 in 1900–01) Goole Town (9–3 in 1914–15) Blackpool (9–2 in 1938–39) and Brighton and Hove Albion (9–0 in 1958–59). 'Boro have netted eight goals at Ayresome Park six times with the last occasion being 20 April 1974 when Sheffield Wednesday were beaten 8–0.

The club's worst home defeat occurred on Christmas Day 1909 when they went down 7–3 to Bradford City whilst 'Boro's highest scoring home match other than those mentioned above is the 7–5 victory over Tottenham Hotspur on 13 February 1915.

HOME SEASONS

Though Middlesbrough have never gone through a league season with an undefeated home record, they have on six occasions lost just once at Ayresome Park - 1901–02, 1926–27, 1936–37, 1968–69, 1971–72 and 1973–74. The club's highest number of home wins in a league season is 18 in 1926–27 when they won the Second Division Championship.

HONOURS

The major honours won by the club are:

Division One Champions	1994–95		
Runners-Up	1997–98		
Division Two Champions	1926–27	1928–29	1973–74
Runners-Up	1901–02	1991–92	
Division Three Runners-Up	1966–67	1986–87	
FA Cup Runners-Up	1997		
League Cup Runners-Up	1997	1998	
FA Amateur Cup Winners	1895	1898	
Anglo-Scottish Cup Winners	1976		
Zenith Data Cup Runners-Up	1990		

HORNER, BILLY

A no-nonsense wing-half, Billy Horner made his Middlesbrough debut in a 1–1 draw at Leyton Orient in March 1961, though it was midway through the 1962–63 season before he won a regular place in the side. He missed very few games over the next six seasons, being ever-present

in 1966–67 when the club won promotion from the Third Division. He had appeared in 217 League and Cup games for 'Boro when manager Stan Anderson transferred him to Darlington in the summer of 1969.

He spent five seasons with the Quakers, appearing in 218 league games before leaving to manage Hartlepool United. In his first two seasons in charge, the club had to seek re-election but improved to finish ninth in 1980–81. After leaving the Victoria Ground in March 1983, he worked as a coach with York City but towards the end of the year he returned to Hartlepool for a second spell in charge. His best season as manager was 1985–86 when 'Pool finished seventh but early the following season he lost his job and took over the reins at Seaham Red Star.

HOWIE, JIMMY

Known as 'Gentleman Jim', Howie played his early football with his home-town club Galston Athletic before joining Kilmarnock in 1899. He later played for both Kettering Town and Bristol Rovers before he signed for Newcastle United in the summer of 1903.

It was at St James Park where his career really took off, his unusual running action concealing his speed, giving him the appearance of strolling through a game. Howie was a great maker and taker of goals and with the Magpies won League Championship medals in 1905, 1907 and 1909 and an FA Cup winners' medal in 1910 when Newcastle beat Everton in the final. After scoring 83 goals in 235 games he left St James Park to play non-League football for Huddersfield Town.

Howie began his managerial career with Queen's Park Rangers, taking them to the FA Cup quarter-final in 1913–14. He left the club just before they joined the Football League to take over the reins at Ayresome Park as successor to Tom McIntosh. After finishing eighth in Division One in each of his first two seasons in charge, the club began to struggle and after they had ended the 1922–23 campaign in 18th position, Howie was released of his duties.

I

INJURIES

The risk of serious injury is an ever-present threat in the game of football and all professional players expect to miss games through injury at some point in their careers.

Steve Corden the son of Middlesbrough director Dick Corden, made his first team debut against Wimbledon at Plough Lane on the opening day of the 1985–86 season. Sadly the 'Boro defender broke his leg just before half-time and never played again. For the record, 'Boro lost 3–0.

One of the most unusual injuries to befall a 'Boro player occurred on 7 February 1987 during the club's Third Division promotion-winning season. As full-back Brian Laws stepped up to take a penalty in the match against Bristol Rovers, he severely damaged his knee ligaments in his run-up and was out for most of the season. Middlesbrough still won 1–0, courtesy of a Stuart Ripley goal.

INTERNATIONAL MATCHES

There have been three international matches involving England played at Ayresome Park plus another three group matches in the 1966 World Cup. The first international played at Ayresome Park on 25 February 1905, saw England draw 1–1 with Ireland. The two countries met again on 14 February 1914 but England with 'Boro's George Elliott in their side lost 3–0. The last international match involving England to be played at Ayresome Park was on 17 November 1937 when goals from

Hall and Matthews helped them beat Wales 2–1 in front of a 50,500 crowd.

In July 1966, Ayresome Park staged three Group Four World Cup games. The results were as follows:

12 July	USSR 3	North Korea 0
15 July	Chile 1	North Korea 1
19 July	Italy 0	North Korea 1

INTERNATIONAL PLAYERS

Middlesbrough's most capped player (ie: caps gained while players were registered with the club) is Wilf Mannion with 26 caps. The following is a complete list of players who have gained full international honours for England, Scotland, Wales, Northern Ireland and the Republic of Ireland:

England

David Armstrong	1
Nick Barmby	8
Ralph Birkett	1
Steve Bloomer	2
George Camsell	9
Jackie Carr	2
Brian Clough	2
Alf Common	1
George Elliott	3
Micky Fenton	1
Paul Gascoigne	3
George Hardwick	13
Eddie Holliday	3
Mick McNeil	9
Wilf Mannion	26
Paul Merson	5
Gary Pallister	2
Alan Peacock	4
John Peacock	3
Billy Pease	1
Fred Pentland	5
Tommy Urwin	3

England (continued)

Maurice Webster	3
Tim Williamson	7

Scotland

Andy Aitken	3
Bob Baxter	3
Billy Brown	1
Bobby Bruce	1
Dave Cumming	1
Stewart Davidson	1
Jock Marshall	6
John Milne	2
Graeme Souness	3
James Stewart	1
Jimmy Watson	2
Derek Whyte	6
Andy Wilson	6

Wales

Clayton Blackmore	1
Albert Davies	1
Tom Griffiths	6

Wales (continued)

Bill Harris	6
John Love Jones	1
Ben Lewis	2
John Mahoney	13
Mel Nurse	3
Fred Warren	3
Joe Williams	1

Northern Ireland

Bobby Braithwaite	7
Terry Cochrane	19
Johnny Crossan	1
Eric McMordie	21
Joe Miller	3
Jim Platt	20

Republic of Ireland

Peter Desmond	4
Arthur Fitzsimons	25
Curtis Fleming	10
James Hartnett	2
Alan Kernaghan	7
Alan Moore	8
Chris Morris	1
Bernie Slaven	7
Andy Townsend	3

The first Middlesbrough player to be capped was Ben Lewis who played for Wales v Scotland in 1893.

J

JACK, DAVID

Though David Jack is perhaps most famous for scoring the first goal in a Wembley Cup Final as Bolton Wanderers beat West Ham United 2–0 in 1923, he contributed far more to the game than that.

He began his career at Plymouth Argyle where his father was the manager. Arsenal and Chelsea, with whom he had played during the First World War, wanted him but he chose his home-town team and signed for Bolton in December 1920. For the next seven seasons he shared the goalscoring responsibilities with Joe Smith and was the club's top league scorer in five of them, with a best return of 26 goals in 1924–25. David Jack netted in six of Bolton's seven FA Cup ties on the way to winning the trophy in 1923. A year later he won the first of four England caps while at Burnden Park but in October 1928 after having scored 161 goals in 324 games he joined Arsenal for a then record £10,340.

Whilst with the Gunners he won both League Championship and FA Cup winners' medals. His first position as a League club manager was with Southend United in 1934 but during his six years in charge at Roots Hall he found it a constant struggle just to keep the club in business. In November 1944 he was appointed manager of Middlesbrough, a season when the club were playing wartime League North football. At Ayresome Park, his best season was 1950–51 when 'Boro finished sixth in the First Division. Some members of the board felt that Jack was too

relaxed and lacked the forceful personality needed to motivate players. In April 1952, Jack resigned his post as manager to become a publican in Islington. He later returned to the game as manager of Shelbourne before taking a job with the Air Ministry.

JANKOVIC, BOSCO

Yugoslavian international Bosco Jankovic joined Middlesbrough from Zeljeznicar in February 1979 and made his debut as a substitute for Micky Burns in a 1–1 draw at Bristol City. After two more appearances as a substitute, he started the game at Bolton which ended goalless before netting his first goal for the club in a 3–0 win at Derby County. Able to play in all of the forward positions, he scored 'Boro's third goal in their 3–1 win at Tottenham Hotspur on the opening day of the 1979–80 season though his best season in terms of goals scored was 1980–81. That campaign saw Jankovic top the club's scoring charts with 12 goals in 23 games but following John Neal's dismissal as 'Boro manager, the Yugoslav who had scored 18 goals in 62 games was allowed to return to his homeland, though the Teeside club held on to his registration.

When Neal was manager of Chelsea, he tried to persuade Jankovic to

Bosco Jankovic

86

join the Stamford Bridge club but he was unsuccessful in his bid. Jankovic stayed in Yugoslavia and in 1994 he died at the tragically young age of 43.

JENNINGS, JACK

Jack Jennings began his Football League career with Wigan Borough before moving to South Wales to play for Cardiff City. His form for the Bluebirds led to him winning selection for the FA touring party of 1926. In January 1930 along with Joe Hillier he was transferred to Middlesbrough and despite going down 4–1 at Leicester City in his first game in Middlesbrough colours, Jennings went on to be a first team regular at Ayresome Park for the next six seasons. In fact, Jennings captained Middlesbrough for much of that time before handing over the leadership duties to Tom Griffiths following his arrival from Bolton Wanderers.

Jennings scored 10 goals in 205 games for 'Boro before leaving to play for Preston North End. He made 19 league appearances for the Deepdale club before moving to Northampton Town. After ending his league career at the County Ground he stayed with the Cobblers as their trainer, a position he later held with the England Amateur international team.

JOHNSTON, CRAIG

Born in Johannesburg, South Africa, Craig Johnston spent his early days in Australia where he played for Lake McQuarrie and Sydney City. After seeing Middlesbrough play in Australia, he decided to try his luck in England and went immediately to Ayresome Park for a trial. He was initially unsuccessful but tried again the following year and was finally taken on by Middlesbrough.

He made his first team debut in a 2–1 win at Birmingham City in February 1978 though he only made 12 appearances over the next couple of seasons. He established himself in the Middlesbrough side in 1979–80, his performances earning him international recognition for England Under-21s, whom he opted for ahead of Australia and Scotland. Johnston, who scored 16 goals in 78 games for 'Boro left Ayresome Park in April 1981, following Graeme Souness to Liverpool in a £580,000 deal.

Unmistakable with his long bushy hair, Johnston soon became an integral part of a Liverpool side that completely dominated English football throughout the 1980s.

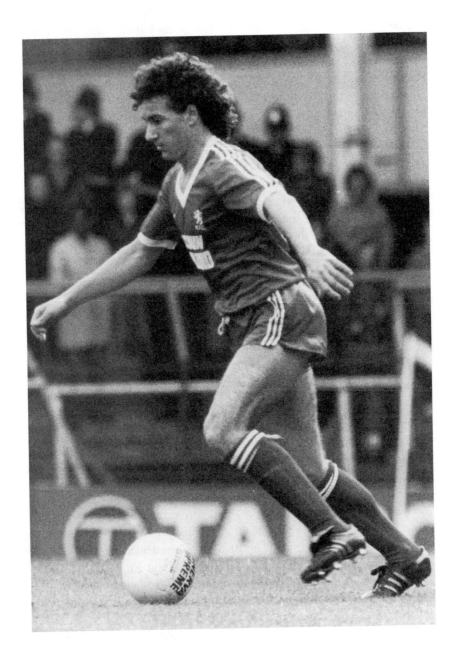

Craig Johnston

He could also score goals, perhaps none more important than the one that put Liverpool ahead in the 1986 FA Cup Final against Everton which the Reds went on to win 3–1. He won a European Cup winners' medal in 1984 plus five League Championship medals as well as an FA Cup winners' medal.

A serious accident to his sister led to his eventual retirement and Johnston who had scored 39 goals in 250 League and Cup games, returned home to Australia at the end of the 1987–88 season to look after her and pursue his other interest, photography.

He later had a spell as a journalist before designing the successful Adidas Predator football boot.

JONES, GORDON

Nobody has made more first team appearances for Middlesbrough since the Second World War than left-back Gordon Jones. He made his debut in January 1961 in a 3–2 defeat at Southampton, replacing Derek Stone-house who was taken ill on the way down to the south coast. Thereafter, Jones missed very few games in 13 seasons with the Ayresome Park club, being ever-present in 1965–66, 1966–67 and 1969–70.

Jones won nine caps for England at Under-23 level and was never on the losing side. He never won full international honours but came very close to selection for Alf Ramsey's World Cup squad of 1966.

When Ian Gibson left to join Coventry City, Jones took over the cap-taincy and skippered the side to promotion to the Second Division in 1966–67. Jones went on to appear in 532 League and Cup games for 'Boro after being granted a testimonial in 1969. When he left Ayresome Park he joined Darlington and made 85 league appearances for the Quakers before ending his playing career with Crook Town, for whom he played on a tour of India.

JUBILEE FUND

The League Benevolent Fund was launched in 1938, fifty years after the start of the Football League, to help players who had fallen on hard times. It was decided that the best way to raise funds was for sides to play local derby games without taking into account league status. Just before the start of the 1938–39 season, Middlesbrough and Sunderland shared six goals before a disappointing attendance of 8,000. Micky Fenton scored two of 'Boro's goals with Benny Yorston netting the other.

JUNINHO

One of the most gifted players in the world, Juninho - real name Oswaldo Giroldo Junior was rejected by Juventus of Brazil before becoming an amateur with Corinthians. After moving to play for Ituano, his performances brought him to the attention of Sao Paulo whom he helped win the World Club Championship in 1994.

The following year, Juninho, who has made 35 full international appearances for Brazil, was voted the Brazilian Footballer of the Year. He came to Bryan Robson's attention when he scored a marvellous goal for Brazil against England at Wembley and though Arsenal made a late bid for his services, it was Middlesbrough who signed him for £4.75 million in November 1995.

He made his debut for 'Boro in a 1–1 draw at home to Leeds United after almost 5,000 fans had turned out to welcome him on the day he arrived at the Riverside Stadium. Though he struggled to produce his best form in his first season with the club, 1996–97 saw him display his skills with great consistency. His goals helped 'Boro to both the FA Cup and League Cup Finals but following the disastrous end of season results, Juninho, who had scored 17 goals in 74 games left the Riverside to join Atletico Madrid for £12 million.

In September 1999 he rejoined Middlesbrough on loan, taking his tally of goals to 21 in 106 games for the Teeside club.

K

KAYE, ARTHUR

Barnsley-born Arthur Kaye played for England Schoolboys before beginning his league career with his home-town club. His early performances for the Oakwell club led to the 5ft 3ins winger winning international recognition for England at Under-23 level and playing for the Football League. He went on to appear in 265 games for Barnsley before leaving to join Blackpool in May 1959.

Seen as the ideal replacement for Stanley Matthews, Kaye found his opportunities at Bloomfield Road limited as the 'Wizard of Dribble' just kept on going. He had appeared in 52 League and Cup games for the Seasiders when Middlesbrough paid £10,000 to bring him to Ayresome Park in November 1960.

He made his debut for 'Boro in a 1–1 home draw against Lincoln City and was the club's first-choice right-winger for the next five seasons. The club's regular penalty-taker, he was a consistent goalscorer, netting 44 in 185 games for the club.

On leaving Ayresome Park, he joined Colchester United, the Layer Road club just having been relegated to the Fourth Division. He made 49 league appearances for the U's before hanging up his boots.

KERNAGHAN, ALAN

Otley-born defender Alan Kernaghan made his Middlesbrough debut as a substitute for Irving Nattrass in a 2–1 home defeat by Oldham

Athletic in February 1985. It was his only appearance that season, followed by just two starts in 1985–86 when 'Boro were relegated to the Third Division. Kernaghan helped the club win promotion at the first attempt before winning a regular place in 1987–88 when 'Boro won promotion for a second successive season. He spent the majority of his first season in the top flight on the bench before returning to the heart of the Middlesbrough defence for the 1989–90 season.

Kernaghan was in outstanding form in 1991–92 as 'Boro won promotion to the newly-formed Premier League as runners-up to Ipswich Town. He couldn't prevent the club losing their top flight status after just one season in the Premiership and in September 1993 after scoring 22 goals in 268 games he joined Manchester City for £1.6 million.

A Republic of Ireland international, he was brought in to strengthen a City squad hit by long term injuries. Though he went on to play in 78 games for the Maine Road club over four seasons, he was second choice behind Curle and Vonk for most of his spell there. He had loan spells with Bolton Wanderers, Bradford City and St Johnstone before joining the Scottish club on a permanent basis just before Christmas 1997.

KINDER, VLADIMIR

The strong-running left-sided defender began his career with his hometown club, Slovan Bratislava, helping them win three consecutive Slovakian league titles. His performances not only helped Bratislava into European competition but led to him winning international recognition for Czechoslovakia and Slovakia. Voted his country's Player of the Year for three years running, he joined Middlesbrough for £1 million in January 1997.

He made his 'Boro debut in an FA Cup tie against non-League Hednesford Town and scored his first goal for the club in a 6–1 win over Derby County. Unfortunately his first season on Teeside will be remembered for his dismissal in the FA Cup semi-final clash against Chesterfield.

In 1997–98 he helped 'Boro return to the top flight at the first time of asking and though he spent much of the 1998–99 campaign on the bench, his strike against Coventry City in 'Boro's 2–1 win over the Sky Blues will long be remembered by a player who has scored five goals in 49 games for the Teeside club.

KNOWLES, CYRIL

Born in the same mining village as England and Yorkshire cricketer Geoff Boycott, he had a year on the junior staff at Manchester United before being released. Middlesbrough recognised that whilst he might not be good enough to make the grade as a winger, he had considerable promise as a full-back and took him on their staff as an amateur. Offered professional terms by 'Boro manager Bob Dennison, he made his first team debut in a 3–3 draw at Derby County in April 1963. Despite preferring to play at left-back, Knowles made most of his 39 first team appearances for the Ayresome Park club at right-back.

In May 1964, Spurs' boss Bill Nicholson paid 'Boro £45,000 for his services. He won his first England Under-23 cap against Wales in November 1964 and at the end of that season played for Young England against England in the annual eve of FA Cup Final match. Knowles was a member of the Spurs' team that won the FA Cup in 1967, the League Cup in 1971 and 1973 and the UEFA Cup in 1972. He won four full caps for England and went on to become a national cult figure due to the success of the pop record 'Nice One Cyril' the title of which became a national catchphrase. Injury forced his retirement from the game after 569 appearances for the White Hart Lane club.

After a short spell as coach to Doncaster Rovers, he returned to Ayresome Park as assistant-manager to Bobby Murdoch before taking over the reins at Darlington. After four years at the Feethams he became manager of Torquay United and took the Devon club to the Sherpa Van Trophy Final in 1989 before becoming boss of Hartlepool United. In February 1991 he faced the shattering diagnosis that he was suffering from a serious brain illness and he died six months later.

L

LARGEST CROWD

It was on 27 December 1949 that Ayresome Park housed its largest crowd. The occasion was the First Division match against Newcastle United. A staggering crowd of 53,596 saw 'Boro win 1–0 courtesy of a Peter McKennan goal.

LATE FINISHES

Middlesbrough's final match of the season against Norwich City on 21 May 1963 is the latest date for the finish of any of 'Boro's seasons. The Canaries were beaten 6–2 with Alan Peacock scoring two of the goals. During the Second World War many curious things occurred, among them the continuance of the 1939–40 season into June. Middlesbrough's last competitive match that campaign saw them beat York City 6–1 on 5 June 1940 with Stobbart scoring four of the goals.

LAWRENCE, LENNIE

In his eight years as manager of Charlton Athletic, Lennie Lawrence experienced just about everything. As well as promotion and relegation, the London club nearly went bankrupt, lost their Valley ground, shared with Crystal Palace and won an exciting play-off match to avoid relegation.

In June 1991 with Charlton on the point of returning to the Valley, Lawrence resigned to take the manager's job at Ayresome Park. It is

questionable however how long he would have lasted at Charlton had he stayed.

Lawrence took Middlesbrough to promotion to the newly-formed Premier League at the end of his first season in charge. They finished as runners-up to Ipswich Town and also reached the semi-finals of the League Cup. Relegated at the end of the 1992–93 season, Lawrence lost his job in May 1994 after the club had ended the campaign in ninth place in the First Division.

Three weeks later he was invited to manage Bradford City. Feeling that he had to recruit new players he spent £1.5 million, but at the end of his first season at the club, City finished 14th following a disastrous end to the season when they won just one of their last 12 games. In November 1995, Lawrence lost his job but the following month he was appointed manager of Luton Town, leading the Hatters to the Second Division play-offs in 1996–97.

LAWS, BRIAN

After joining Burnley, Brian Law's progress at Turf Moor was rapid for this determined young footballer who made his league debut in the final game of the club's relegation season of 1979–80. Over the next three seasons he was the Clarets' first choice right-back. In 1981–82 he experienced the triumph of the Third Division Championship but following the club's relegation the following season he left to join Huddersfield Town.

His stay at Leeds Road was brief and in March 1985, Willie Maddren took the Wallsend-born player to Middlesbrough. He made his debut in a 1–0 home win over Sheffield United and played in the last 11 games of the campaign, scoring his first goal for the club in a 2–0 win at Shrewsbury on the final day of the season. After a relegation and two successive promotions at Ayresome Park, Laws stood on the brink of top flight football but after scoring 14 goals in 124 games, he was allowed to join Brian Clough's Nottingham Forest.

He ended his first season at the City Ground with a Littlewoods Cup Winners' medal and a Simod Cup winners' medal. Another Littlewoods Cup medal followed in 1990. He went on to appear in 209 League and Cup games for Forest before moving to Grimsby Town as player-manager. He left Blundell Park in 1996 and is currently in charge of Scunthorpe United.

LEADING GOALSCORERS

Middlesbrough have provided the Football League's divisional leading goalscorer on eight occasions:

They are:

1913–14	George Elliott	Division One	31 goals
1921–22	Andy Wilson	Division One	31 goals
1926–27	George Camsell	Division Two	59 goals
1958–59	Brian Clough	Division Two	42 goals
1959–60	Brian Clough	Division Two	39 goals
1967–68	John Hickton	Division Two	24 goals
1969–70	John Hickton	Division Two	24 goals
1970–71	John Hickton	Division Two	25 goals

LEAGUE GOALS - CAREER HIGHEST

George Camsell holds the Middlesbrough record for the most league goals with a career total of 326 between 1925 and 1939.

LEAGUE GOALS - LEAST CONCEDED

Middlesbrough conceded just 30 goals in seasons 1973–74 and 1986–87, winning promotion on each occasion as Second Division champions and Third Division runners-up respectively.

LEAGUE GOALS - MOST INDIVIDUAL

George Camsell holds the Middlesbrough record for the most league goals in a season with 59 scored in 1926–27 when the club won the Second Division Championship. The total remains a Second Division record.

LEAGUE GOALS - MOST SCORED

Middlesbrough's highest goal tally in the Football League was in the Second Division Championship-winning season of 1926–27 when they scored 122 goals.

LEAGUE VICTORY - HIGHEST

Middlesbrough's best Football League victory was the 10–3 win over Sheffield United at Ayresome Park on 18 November 1933. George Camsell scored four of the goals and Bobby Bruce a hat-trick. The other scorers were Charlie Ferguson, Freddie Warren and Bob Baxter. 'Boro

have scored nine goals in a league match on three occasions - Gainsborough Trinity (9–2 on 2 March 1901) Blackpool (9–2 on 10 December 1938) and Brighton and Hove Albion (9–0 on 23 August 1958).

LINACRE, BILL

Speedy winger Bill Linacre broke his leg three times in a league career that began with his hometown club Chesterfield in 1944. In fact, Linacre broke his leg twice whilst playing for the Spireites. He made a full recovery and in October 1947 joined Manchester City to assist the Maine Road club on their return to the First Division. He had made 75 appearances for City when Middlesbrough manager David Jack paid £18,000 to take Linacre to Ayresome Park.

He made his debut for 'Boro in a 3–0 win at Charlton Athletic in September 1949 and scored his only goal of that campaign in a 4–1 home win over Burnley. In February 1950 he broke his leg for a third time in 'Boro's 1–0 win against his former club Manchester City at Maine Road. He returned to first team action towards the end of the following season but made just five appearances. In 1951–52 he played in the club's opening four games but wasn't the player he was and left the club to play non-League football for Goole Town.

He later returned to league action with Hartlepool United and scored 10 goals in 89 games before joining Mansfield Town where he ended his league career. Later he had another spell of non-League football, playing for Blyth Spartans.

LONG SERVICE

The club's longest-serving player is goalkeeper Tim Williamson who appeared in 602 League and Cup games from 1902 to 1923. Other long-serving players include Jackie Carr (1910–1930) and George Camsell (1925–1943, after which he served the club as chief scout, coach and assistant-secretary).

LOWEST

The lowest number of goals scored by Middlesbrough in a single Football League season is 34 in 1981–82. The club's lowest points total in the Football League occurred in 1923–24 when 'Boro gained just 22 points from 42 matches when they finished bottom of the First Division.

M

McANDREW, TONY

A Scottish Youth international, Tony McAndrew joined Middlesbrough in the summer of 1971 but had to wait until November 1973 before making his first appearance for the club. Replacing the injured Graeme Souness, he made one of the goals in a 2–1 win over Luton Town. That was McAndrew's only first team appearance that season as the club won the Second Division Championship. He made just one appearance again in 1974–75 before winning a regular first team spot towards the end of the 1975–76 campaign. That season he appeared in a variety of positions, but on 17 April 1976 whilst playing at centre-forward, he netted a hat-trick in a 3–0 win over Sheffield United.

During the close season, McAndrew played for Vancouver Whitecaps in the NASL before returning to the Middlesbrough side. Following Stuart Boam's departure to Newcastle United, manager John Neal made him club captain.

When 'Boro were relegated in 1981–82, McAndrew decided that he still wanted to play top flight football and so joined his former boss John Neal at Chelsea. The Ayresome Park club had asked for £300,000 but an independent tribunal set the fee at £92,500. He spent just two seasons at Stamford Bridge before rejoining Middlesbrough managed by Willie Maddren in September 1984. He helped to shore up 'Boro's defence for another two seasons but following the club's relegation to the Third Division in 1985–86 McAndrew, who had scored 18 goals in

358 games left the first-class game.

He played non-League football for Willington before making a surprise return to league action with Hartlepool United. He later coached Darlington, Leicester City and Aston Villa.

Tony McAndrew

McCLELLAND, JIMMY

After beginning his career with Raith Rovers, Jimmy McClelland came south of the border to play for Southend United in 1923.

At Southend he led the scoring charts during 1924–25 with 16 goals in 23 games but in March 1925 he moved to Ayresome Park.

His first game for the club came in a goalless draw at Hull City before he scored on his home debut in a 2–0 win over Sheffield Wednesday. In 1925–26 McClelland was the club's top scorer with 38 goals in 40 games including all five in a 5–1 FA Cup win over Leeds United and hat-tricks in the wins over Wolves (Home 4–1), Blackpool (Away 3–2), and Portsmouth (Home 4–1). Though he was somewhat overshadowed by George Camsell's goalscoring exploits in 1926–27, he played his part in helping 'Boro win the Second Division Championship. McClelland had scored 48 goals in 85 games for Middlesbrough when, in March 1928, he was allowed to join Bolton Wanderers for £6,300.

He scored on his debut for the Trotters in a 2–2 draw at Burnley and scored eight goals in the last ten games of the season. He won an FA Cup winners' medal in 1929 as Bolton beat Portsmouth 2–0 in the Wembley final but early the following season he left to join Preston North End. His stay at Deepdale was brief as he returned to the First Division with Blackpool. He remained at Bloomfield Road until 1933 before having a short spell with Bradford prior to ending his league career with Manchester United who had just won promotion to the First Division.

McCRAE, ALEX

After beginning his career with Heart of Midlothian, inside-left Alex McCrae came south of the border in the summer of 1947 to join Charlton Athletic for a fee of £7,500. His stay at the Valley was brief and after turning down an offer to join Sheffield United, signed for Middlesbrough for £10,000 in October 1948.

He made his debut the following month in a 2–0 defeat at Derby County and though he lost his place in the side after seven appearances, he soon rediscovered his form to help 'Boro fight off relegation. He went on to be a first team regular at Ayresome Park for five seasons with his best campaign being 1950–51 when he scored 21 goals in 32 games to help 'Boro finish sixth in Division One. Included in his total were hat-tricks against Everton (Home 4–0), Huddersfield Town (Home 8–0), and Blackpool (Home 4–3). He went on to score 49 goals in 130 games before joining Falkirk. He later became player-coach of Ballymena United before managing both Stirling Albion and Falkirk.

McILMOYLE, HUGH

Much travelled centre-forward Hugh McIlmoyle began his career with Port Glasgow before joining Leicester City in 1959 and playing in the

FA Cup Final of 1961. He then moved via Rotherham United to Carlisle United in March 1963 and was the Cumbrian side's leading marksman in their 1963–64 promotion success and FA Cup run. He joined Wolverhampton Wanderers in October 1964 for a fee of £30,000. Despite the club being relegated at the end of McIlmoyle's first season at Molineux, he had scored 14 goals in 32 games including a hat-trick in a 3–1 FA Cup fifth second replay against Aston Villa. He continued to find the back of the net with great regularity and in 1965–66, scored 17 goals in 44 games. Yet midway through the following season he was allowed to lave Molineux and joined Bristol City. Unable to settle at Ashton Gate he rejoined Carlisle United for a cut-price £22,000. In 1968–69 he was ever-present and top-scorer but after two years in his second spell at Brunton Park, he moved to Middlesbrough where he linked up well with John Hickton.

After making his debut in a 2–0 home defeat by Blackpool in September 1969, he went on to end the campaign with six goals in 29 games. In 1970–71 he took his tally of goals for 'Boro to 22 in 82 League and Cup games but was surprisingly released at the end of the season in which the club had finished seventh in Division Two. He later played for Preston North End and Morton before returning to Carlisle for a third spell after which he ended his career. He had been a professional for 16 years during which time he had scored 153 league goals in 446 games for his seven clubs.

McINTOSH, TOM

Tom McIntosh began his career with Darlington where after seven seasons he was offered the secretary's job. The Feethams club turned professional in 1908 and in 1910–11 had a good run in that season's FA Cup, beating league clubs Sheffield United and Bradford.

Following Andy Walker's suspension for bribery, Tom McIntosh was offered and accepted the post of Middlesbrough's secretary-manager. In 1913–14 he guided 'Boro to third place in the First Division, their highest-ever league placing. After the club had finished 12th the following season, war brought an end to a successful period, when the club closed down. In August 1914 McIntosh had joined the Teeside Pioneers and later saw active service as a sergeant in France. He led 'Boro to the Northern Victory League title in 1919 but then accepted an offer to join Everton as secretary without team responsibilities and he remained at Goodison Park until his death in October 1935.

McMORDIE, ERIC

Spotted by Manchester United as a youngster, Eric McMordie had a short trial at Old Trafford at the same time as George Best, but both returned to Ireland after feeling homesick. Though Sir Matt Busby asked both boys to return, McMordie decided to stay in Ireland and turned out as an amateur for the Dundela club.

Following a recommendation to 'Boro boss Raich Carter, McMordie signed professional forms for Middlesbrough in September 1964 but had to wait until the 1965–66 season before making his debut. His first game was against Plymouth Argyle, McMordie laying on both 'Boro goals in a 2–2 draw. He ended the season with four goals in 17 games but 'Boro were relegated to the Third Division. They bounced straight back the following season, but McMordie only made 19 appearances and it was midway through 1967–68 before he won a regular place.

At the start of the following season, McMordie won the first of 21 full caps for Northern Ireland when he played against Israel in Jaffa.

Following the arrival of Jack Charlton as manager, McMordie's services were no longer required and after scoring 26 goals in 277 games he was loaned out to Sheffield Wednesday. Despite an impressive nine-match spell at Hillsborough in which he scored six goals, nothing came of the move and he signed for York City. After making 42 league appearances for the Minstermen he moved to Hartlepool United where he ended his league career at the early age of 31 after playing in a further 46 league games.

McNEIL, MICK

Middlesbrough-born Mick McNeil began his league career with his home-town club, making his debut in a 6–4 win at Brighton and Hove Albion in December 1958. His early appearances for the club were at left-half but on losing his place to Ray Yeoman he switched to full-back. In 1959–60, McNeil was ever-present as 'Boro finished fifth in Division Two. He was selected for an FA XI against the Army at St James Park and followed this up with a number of appearances for the England Under-23 side.

His performances in the Middlesbrough defence led to him winning full international honours when he played for England against Ireland in Belfast. Eight further caps soon followed but in the summer of 1964 after appearing in 193 games for 'Boro he was allowed to join Ipswich Town.

Although he did not add to his international caps whilst at Portman Road, he did captain an FA XI to a 10–0 win over Jersey in a match played to commemorate the centenary of the Jersey FA.

He played the last of his 173 League and Cup games for Ipswich in February 1972 before entering non-League football with Cambridge City.

McWILLIAM, PETER

Born in Inverness in 1879, Peter McWilliam started his football career with local side Heatherley before joining Inverness Thistle. In 1902 he signed for Newcastle United and went straight into the Magpies' league side for their match against Middlesbrough. However, in his first game in Newcastle's colours he was on the losing side as 'Boro won 1–0. He was dropped for the next game but soon won a regular place in the Newcastle side, going on to appear in 240 games over the next seven seasons. With the Magpies he won three League Championship medals and also won an FA Cup winners' medal against Barnsley in 1910 after picking up three runners-up medals. He made his Scotland debut against England at the Crystal Palace in April 1905 but received a knee injury against Wales in March 1911 which ultimately ended his playing career.

In May 1913 he was appointed manager of Tottenham Hotspur but they were relegated in 1914–15 and had to wait four years before they had the chance of returning to the top flight. In 1919–20 Spurs ran away with the Second Division title and in 1921 won the FA Cup. In 1921–22 they finished runners-up in the First Division but after this they went into decline. He was in the process of rebuilding the team at White Hart Lane when he was approached by Middlesbrough about becoming boss of the Ayresome Park club. They offered him £1,500 per annum which was £200 more than Spurs were paying him. After asking for a rise and being refused, he handed in his notice at White Hart Lane and joined 'Boro as manager in April 1927.

At Ayresome Park, McWilliam was given complete control of team selection without any interference from the board. Though 'Boro went on to win the Second Division title that season, McWilliam found it difficult to win over the fans, whose sympathy lay with Herbert Bamlett who was sacked after leading the club to the top of the table!

'Boro were relegated the following season but returned to the top flight as Second Division champions again in 1928–29. McWilliam was sacked in March 1934 and then scouted for Arsenal before returning to White Hart Lane to manage Spurs for a second time. His stay was brief,

though he was instrumental in establishing the famous Northfleet Nursery which produced a number of fine players for Spurs.

MACKIE, ALEX

An administrator who never played professional football, Alex Mackie was associated with a number of Scottish clubs before becoming Sunderland's third manager in the summer of 1899.

Despite starting the 1899–1900 season with eight wins and a draw out of their opening 11 games, the Wearsiders' form slumped and they had to settle for third place. In 1900–01 the club suffered only six defeats and finished the season as runners-up to Liverpool. In 1901–02 Sunderland won the League Championship and the following season were third, just a point behind champions Sheffield Wednesday.

In 1903, the FA investigated Sunderland's books after Andy McCombie claimed that the Wearsiders had paid him £100 to start a business. The club said that the payment had been a loan but when the books were examined, irregularities were found. Alex Mackie was banned for three months but when he did return to the club, he sold Alf Common to Middlesbrough for £1,000, the first four-figure transfer fee in the history of the game. Soon afterwards, Mackie followed Common to Ayresome Park as Middlesbrough's manager.

He signed the legendary Steve Bloomer in March 1906 but once again accusations began to fly and again the FA were called in to look into the matter. Illegal payments had again been made to players and books not kept properly. Suspended for a second time, the disillusioned Mackie left the game to run a pub in Middlesbrough.

MADDREN, WILLIE

Just two days before he was due to have a trial with Leeds United, Willie Maddren broke his ankle whilst playing for Port Clarence Juniors. The Elland Road club never followed up their interest and Middlesbrough stepped in to offer him professional terms in the summer of 1968.

Maddren made his league debut for 'Boro as a forward in the last home game of the 1968–69 season and scored in a 3–2 defeat by Bury. It was the 1970–71 season before he established himself as a first team regular, ending the campaign as the club's Player of the Year. One of the club's most versatile players, Maddren played in seven different positions before forming a formidable central defensive partnership with Stuart Boam. His performances led to him winning five England Under-23 caps

but he never gained full honours his displays deserved.

Sadly, Maddren's career was brought to a premature end at the age of 26, when he damaged his knee in a 2–1 defeat at West Bromwich Albion in September 1977. Maddren, who had scored 21 goals in 354 games, joined Hartlepool as coach but returned to Ayresome Park in 1983 as coach and physiotherapist. Following Jack Charlton's decision to leave the club, Maddren was made manager on the former Leeds and England centre-half's recommendation.

The former 'Boro defender faced an uphill struggle to turn things round, as the club were already £1.2 million in debt. In February 1986 he was sacked and replaced by Bruce Rioch. On leaving the club he returned to running his successful sports shops in the area.

Willie Maddren

MANAGERS

This is a complete list of Middlesbrough's full-time managers with the inclusive dates during which they held office:

John Robson	1899–1905	Raich Carter	1963–1966
Alex Mackie	1905–1906	Stan Anderson	1966–1973
Andy Aitken	1906–1909	Jack Charlton	1973–1977
Andy Walker	1910–1911	John Neal	1977–1981
Tom McIntosh	1911–1919	Bobby Murdoch	1981–1982
Jimmy Howie	1920–1923	Malcolm Allison	1982–1984
Herbert Bamlett	1923–1927	Willie Maddren	1984–1986
Peter McWilliam	1927–1934	Bruce Rioch	1986–1990
Wilf Gillow	1934–1944	Colin Todd	1990–1991
David Jack	1944–1952	Lennie Lawrence	1991–1994
Walter Rowley	1952–1954	Bryan Robson	1994–
Bob Dennison	1954–1963		

MANNION, WILF

The most famous player in the history of Middlesbrough Football Club, Wilf Mannion was an outstanding schoolboy player, turning out for South Bank before going professional with 'Boro in September 1936. He made his debut for the Ayresome Park club in a 2–2 draw against Portsmouth in January 1937. The following season he became a regular in the 'Boro side, playing First Division football at the age of 17 and when war broke out, he made his first appearance for England. In that last season of League football before the hostilities, Mannion scored 14 goals in 38 games including four in the 9–2 rout of Blackpool and a hat-trick in the 8–2 defeat of Portsmouth.

Mannion was a beautifully balanced player with immaculate close control, a dangerous burst of speed and the ability to weave his team expertly together.

During the war he served in the Middle East and Italy but it didn't seem to have affected his game in any way, for he returned to the England team in Belfast as soon as official internationals were resumed in 1946, scoring a hat-trick in a 7–2 win.

For Middlesbrough he had his best season in terms of goals scored, finishing the 1946–47 campaign as joint-top scorer with Micky Fenton. His total of 23 goals included a hat-trick in a 3–3 draw against Portsmouth. In May 1947 his magnificent performance at Glasgow

against the Rest of Europe established him beyond doubt as a great player. Playing at inside-right, he scored the first goal, then another and would have had a hat-trick had Lawton not touched one of his shots as it was crossing the line. He darted irrepressibly all over the field, pulling the hapless European defence to pieces - it was a marvellous exhibition.

At the beginning of the 1948–49 season, Mannion refused to re-sign for Middlesbrough. For a time he took a demonstrating job outside football but in those days, the clubs held all the aces and Mannion was forced to return to the game with 'Boro, having lost a good deal of money in wages and missed six internationals. However, he soon regained his place in the England side and went on to play in 26 internationals.

At the end of the 1953–54 season, Mannion, who had scored 110 goals in 368 League and Cup games, decided to retire. However, Hull City paid £5,000 for his signature after persuading Mannion to come out of retirement. He spent just one season with the Boothferry Park club before the Football League suspended him for refusing to give chapter and verse about alleged illegal payments to players.

Mannion then went to play non-League football for Poole Town, King's Lynn, Haverfield Rovers and Earlstown before finally retiring at the age of 44 in 1952. 'Boro are keen to honour Wilf, who died at the age of 81, with a permanent memorial.

MARATHON MATCHES
Middlesbrough have been involved in a number of cup games that have gone to three matches - Willington Athletic (FA Cup 1900–01); Brighton and Hove Albion (FA Cup 1905–06); Charlton Athletic (FA Cup 1929–30); Bolton Wanderers (FA Cup 1938–39); Blackpool (FA Cup 1945–46); Aston Villa (FA Cup 1949–50); Hull City (League Cup 1962–63); York City (FA Cup 1966–67); Hull City (FA Cup 1967–68); Tottenham Hotspur (League Cup 1972–73); and Everton (FA Cup 1987–88).

MARKSMEN - LEAGUE
Middlesbrough's top League goalscorer is George Camsell who struck 325 goals during his time at Ayresome Park. Only seven players have hit more than 100 League goals for the club.

1.	George Camsell	325
2.	George Elliott	203
3.	Brian Clough	197

4.	John Hickton	159
5.	Micky Fenton	147
6.	Alan Peacock	125
7.	Bernie Slaven	118
8.=	Wilf Mannion	99
	Billy Pease	99
10.=	David Mills	90
	Lindy Delapenha	90

MARKSMEN - OVERALL

Ten players have hit a hundred goals for Middlesbrough. The club's top marksman is George Camsell. The Century Club consist of:

1.	George Camsell	345
2.	George Elliott	213
3.	Brian Clough	204
4.	John Hickton	185
5.	Micky Fenton	162
6.	Alan Peacock	141
7.	Bernie Slaven	132
8.	Wilf Mannion	110
9.	David Mills	108
10.	Billy Pease	102

MARSHALL, JOCK

Full-back Jock Marshall joined Middlesbrough from St Mirren for a fee of £1,800 in November 1919 and made his debut that month in a goalless home draw against Chelsea. A virtual ever-present in the 'Boro side for the next four seasons, it was reputed that he could kick the ball the length of the field and though he never scored for the Ayresome Park club, he possessed a very powerful shot.

A Scottish international, he was suspended by the Football League after returning north of the border to take part in a five-a-side competition. He was later suspended by the club for returning to his native country without permission!

Though the suspension was eventually lifted, Marshall, who had played in 121 games, left 'Boro to join Llanelli where he became the only player this century to win full Scottish honours whilst with a non-League club.

MARTIN, JACK

Following an unsuccessful trial with Portsmouth, wing-half Jack Martin played non-League football for Horden Colliery Welfare where he was spotted by 'Boro manager Peter McWilliam. After signing for the Ayresome Park club in March 1932, Martin spent a year in the club's reserve side before being given his first team debut against Blackburn Rovers on the final day of the 1932–33 season. The ball-playing Martin had an outstanding match, helping 'Boro to a 4–0 win. Over the next five seasons, Martin missed very few matches and had appeared in 137 League and Cup games by the time the Second World War broke out.

During the hostilities, Jack Martin played in 130 wartime games but in October 1944 he was badly injured in a 1–1 draw at Bradford City and took almost a year to make a complete recovery. He was later given a free transfer and had spells as trainer with both Huddersfield Town and Doncaster Rovers.

MATCH OF THE DAY

Middlesbrough's first appearance on BBC's 'Match of the Day' was on 7 December 1968 when they drew 1–1 with Blackpool at Bloomfield Road, with Dickie Rooks netting for 'Boro.

MATHIESON, JIMMY

Goalkeeper Jimmy Mathieson began his career with Raith Rovers before signing for Middlesbrough in the summer of 1926 for a fee of £1,200.

He made his 'Boro debut in a 3–0 defeat at Chelsea on the opening day of the 1926–27 season, a campaign in which he was the club's only ever-present as they went on to win the Second Division Championship. Mathieson, who kept 12 clean sheets, also conceded four goals on three occasions in a season in which George Camsell scored 59 goals. He was ever-present again the following campaign as 'Boro suffered relegation after just one season in the top flight. Mathieson appeared in 99 con-secutive League games following his debut before injury forced him to miss two games midway through the 1928–29 season. He returned to keep 13 clean sheets and help the club win the Second Division title for the second time in three years.

Mathieson went on to appear in 264 League and Cup games before leaving Ayresome Park in May 1934 to join Brentford. He helped the Bees win promotion to the First Division before returning north of the border to see out his career with Queen of the South.

MILLS, DAVID

An England Schoolboy international, David Mills signed for Middlesbrough in the summer of 1968 and made his first team debut as a substitute for Stanley Webb in the first game of the 1968–69 season at Birmingham City. He made his full debut at Swindon Town in the final game of the following season, scoring in a 3–0 win. It was midway through the 1971–72 season before Mills established himself as a first team regular, his performances earning him selection for the England Under-23 side. He helped 'Boro win the Second Division Championship in 1973–74, scoring 11 goals in 39 games. He continued to find the net over the next five seasons with a best return of 18 goals in 1976–77 including a hat-trick in a 3–2 home win over Aston Villa. Mills had scored 94 goals in 345 League and Cup games when after asking for a

David Mills

transfer he became Britain's first half-million pound footballer by join-ing West Bromwich Albion.

Albion manager Ron Atkinson saw Mills as the perfect replacement for Tony Brown but he couldn't get into the West Brom side and spent much of his first season at the Hawthorns on the bench. Even when first team regulars Cunningham and Cantello left Albion, Mills damaged an Achilles tendon and wasn't fit enough for contention. After just 55 appearances he left to join Sheffield Wednesday.

That move was not a success but he fared better at Newcastle where he played alongside Kevin Keegan. After being released, he rejoined Middlesbrough, taking his tally of goals to 108 in 381 games before fol-lowing a spell with Darlington, he became player-coach at non-League Whitby Town. It was whilst with Whitby that Mills suffered terrible injuries in a car crash which also killed his father and he was forced to retire from football after a long period in hospital.

MOCHAN, NEIL

After playing his early football for Dunipace Thistle, he joined Morton in April 1944. His performances for the Cappielow Park club led to a number of top clubs showing an interest in his future. It was Middlesbrough who paid £14,000 for his services in the summer of 1951, Mochan playing his first game for the club in the Festival of Britain match against Partizan Belgrade.

Mochan made his League debut for 'Boro in a 2–1 home win over Tottenham Hotspur on the opening day of the 1951–52 season. He went on to score 14 goals in 39 games before surprisingly being allowed to leave Ayresome Park and return north of the border to join Celtic.

Whilst with the Parkhead club he won Scottish League, Scottish Cup and Scottish League Cup Winners' medals, his form also leading to him winning three full caps for Scotland. On leaving Celtic he had spells with Dundee United and Raith Rovers but was back at Parkhead as the club's trainer when they won the European Cup in 1967.

MORRIS, CHRIS

Republic of Ireland international full-back Chris Morris, who was able to play on either flank, began his League career with Sheffield Wednesday. He had appeared in 96 League and Cup games for the Owls when Celtic paid £125,000 to take him to Parkhead.

With Celtic, Morris won a Scottish Premier Division Championship

medal in 1988 and Scottish Cup winners' medals in 1988 and 1989. He had played in 211 games for the Scottish giants when Middlesbrough manager Lennie Lawrence brought him to Ayresome Park in the summer of 1992. He made his Middlesbrough debut in a 2–1 defeat at Coventry City on the opening day of the 1992–93 season, the inaugural campaign of the Premier League. Despite 'Boro's relegation, Morris was in fine form, scoring his first goal for the club in a 2–0 home win over Wimbledon.

A player who always gave 100%, he enjoyed success with 'Boro as a wing/back where his overlapping caused many a problem for the opposition. He had appeared in 104 games for 'Boro when he was released at the end of the 1996–97 season.

MOST GOALS IN A SEASON
Middlesbrough scored 122 goals in 42 Division Two matches during 1926–27. On three occasions they scored seven goals against Portsmouth (Home 7–3), Swansea Town (Home 7–1), and Grimsby Town (Away 7–4), while they managed six on two other occasions. Yet Middlesbrough had managed just one point and scored only one goal in their first four league games. In the fourth game they brought in George Camsell who ended the season as top scorer with 59 goals.

MOST MATCHES
Middlesbrough played their most matches, 60, in the 1991–92 season. This comprised 46 League games, four FA Cup games, eight Football League Cup games and two Zenith Data Systems Cup games.

MOWBRAY, TONY
Tony Mowbray had stood on the Holgate End at Ayresome Park as a youngster, supporting Middlesbrough, so signing schoolboy forms in 1978 was like a dream come true. He progressed through the ranks to make his 'Boro debut in a 1–1 draw at Newcastle United in September 1982.

After establishing himself as a first team regular towards the end of that season, Mowbray missed very few games over the next nine seasons, being ever-present in 1986–87 and 1987–88 when the club went from the Third Division to the top flight in successive promotions. Forming an outstanding central defensive partnership with Gary Pallister, Mowbray won international recognition when he was chosen for the England 'B' tour, playing in all three games against Switzerland, Norway and Iceland.

After the liquidation saga of 1986, Mowbray was appointed the club's captain and had the honour of leading out 'Boro at Wembley in the Zenith Data Systems Cup Final of 1990. In November 1991, Mowbray who had scored 29 goals in 424 games for 'Boro joined Celtic for £1 million. His time at Parkhead was hampered by injuries and after appearing in 96 games in four years he left to sign for Ipswich Town in October 1995 for a fee of £300,000. Appointed captain of the Suffolk club, he has led the side by example, despite missing a number of games through injury.

MURDOCH, BOBBY

Bobby Murdoch was one of Celtic's greatest-ever players, helping the Parkhead club to eight consecutive Scottish League Championships. He also appeared in eight Scottish Cup Finals and another eight Scottish

Bobby Murdoch

League Cup Finals. He was a member of the Celtic team that became the first British club side to win the European Cup in 1967 when Inter Milan were beaten 2–1 in Lisbon. Three years later they lost in the final to Feyenoord 2–1 in Milan, with Murdoch again in the side. After scoring 61 goals in 291 League games for Celtic, Murdoch moved south to join Middlesbrough.

The Scottish international made his 'Boro debut in a goalless draw at Blackpool in September 1973, going on to score five goals in 34 games as the Teeside club won the Second Division Championship. After helping the club consolidate their place in the top flight, Murdoch, who had scored nine goals in 125 games, stayed on at Ayresome Park to coach the club's juniors.

Following the departure of John Neal in May 1981, Bobby Murdoch was appointed Middlesbrough's manager, despite having no previous experience. The loss of star players like David Armstrong and Craig Johnston weakened the side and after the club were relegated to the Second Division in 1981–82, Murdoch was sacked shortly afterwards.

MUSTOE, ROBBIE
Midfielder Robbie Mustoe began his Football League career with his local club, Oxford United. He made his debut against Liverpool in 1987 and though the Manor Ground club were relegated at the end of that season, Mustoe established himself in the Oxford side, scoring 10 goals in 98 games before his £375,000 move to Middlesbrough in the summer of 1990.

Mustoe, who had won England Under-21 honours whilst with Oxford, made his 'Boro debut in a goalless home draw against West Ham United on the opening day of the 1990–91 season. Since then, Mustoe has been an established member of the 'Boro side, playing under three managers in Colin Todd, Lennie Lawrence and present boss, Bryan Robson.

He helped the club win promotion to the Premier League in 1991–92, the First Division Championship in 1994–95 and promotion to the top flight again in 1997–98. Vastly under-rated and one of the club's most consistent players, Robbie Mustoe, who has scored 33 goals in 382 games, continues to command a first team place at the Riverside Stadium.

N

NATTRASS, IRVING

Irving Nattrass began his Football League career with Newcastle United, making his debut for the Magpies as a substitute against Derby County in March 1971.

In nine years with the St James Park club, he appeared in 313 League and Cup games including the League Cup Final of 1976.

His form for the Tyneside club was such that he earned selection for the England Under-23 side but missed out on a possible full cap when injury forced him to withdraw from England's trip to South America in 1977.

Following the Magpies' relegation to the Second Division in 1979, Nattrass wanted to remain in the top flight. 'Boro manager John Neal persuaded the Fishburn-born player to join the Ayresome Park club with an independent tribunal fixing the fee of £475,000 - a club record that lasted until the arrival of Peter Davenport.

Nattrass made his debut for 'Boro in a 2–0 defeat at Arsenal on 15 September 1979 after an Achilles injury had delayed his introduction to the side.

During his first season with the club, Nattrass made only 13 first team appearances as he suffered three hairline fractures of the leg. Thankfully he made a full recovery and went on to appear in nine different positions for the club in his 220 games.

Irving Nattrass

NEAL, JOHN

Signed for Hull City by Raich Carter, John Neal played in 60 League games for the Tigers before signing for Swindon Town in the summer of 1957. Two years later he left the County Ground for Aston Villa and after missing the opening match of the 1959–60 season, played in all the remaining games, winning a Second Division Championship medal. He also won a League Cup winners' tankard in 1961 but a year later he left Villa Park after playing in 114 games to join Southend United.

After his playing days were over, he moved to Wrexham as the Welsh club's first team trainer but when Alvan Williams resigned in September 1968, Neal replaced him. In his first season with the club, they finished ninth in the Fourth Division but in 1969–70 he led them to promotion

as runners-up to Chesterfield. In 1972 the Robins won the Welsh Cup for the first time in 12 years and in 1973–74 he took the club into the sixth round of the FA Cup for the first time in their history. He led the club to another Welsh Cup victory in 1975 but perhaps his best performance as Wrexham manager was to lead the club into the quarter-finals of the European Cup Winners' Cup in 1976. In 1976–77 he almost took the club into the Second Division for the first time in their history but they lost their last two home matches when a draw would have ensured promotion for the club.

He left the Racecourse Ground in May 1977 to take charge at Middlesbrough. Neal instilled an attacking flair in 'Boro's side but he

John Neal

began to sell a number of the players who had flourished under Jack Charlton. He sold Graeme Souness to Liverpool and David Mills to West Bromwich Albion. He left the club after four seasons in charge at Ayresome Park following a disagreement over the sale of Craig Johnston to Liverpool.

He then joined Chelsea and in 1983–84 took the Stamford Bridge club to the Second Division Championship. The following season the Pensioners were fifth in the First Division and reached the semi-finals of the League Cup but he was still replaced by John Hollins and moved 'upstairs' as a member of the board.

NEUTRAL GROUNDS

Ayresome Park was used as a neutral ground for FA Cup matches on a number of occasions and as early as February 1905 staged an international match when England drew 1–1 with Ireland. The ground which was the venue for two further England international matches, also staged three games during the 1966 World Cup competition.

The Football League v the Scottish League fixture was played at Ayresome Park on four occasions, whilst the ground was also the venue for nine FA Amateur Cup Finals, the last occasion being 1962 when Crook Town beat Hounslow Town 4–0.

Middlesbrough themselves have had to replay on a neutral ground on a number of occasions:

Date	Opponents	Venue	FA Cup	Score
12.02.1906	Brighton & H.A.	Bramall Lane	Rd 2	3–1
03.02.1930	Charlton Athletic	Maine Road	Rd 4	1–0
04.02.1946	Blackpool	Elland Road	Rd 4	1–0
16.01.1950	Aston Villa	Elland Road	Rd 3	3–0
16.01.1957	York City	St James Park	Rd 2	4–1
07.02.1968	Hull City	Bootham Crescent	Rd 3	1–0

The club's FA Cup semi-final appearance against Chesterfield in 1996–97 was also played on a neutral ground. Following the 3–3 draw at Old Trafford, the replay which 'Boro won 3–0 was at Hillsborough. The club's appearances in that seasons FA Cup and League Cup Finals at Wembley also qualify for inclusion as does 'Boro's second successive appearance in the League Cup Final in 1998.

NEWCASTLE UNITED

Middlesbrough's first meeting with Newcastle United was in the FA Cup competition of 1892–93 when goals from Black, Blyth and McKnight gave 'Boro a 3–2 win. The clubs met a further three times in the FA Cup over the next few seasons before in 1902–03 they met for the first time in the Football League. On 18 October 1902 'Boro travelled to St James Park and won 1–0 courtesy of a Chris Carrick goal. They completed the 'double' on St Valentine's Day, winning 1–0 with Joe Cassidy the goalscorer.

When the Magpies visited Ayresome Park on 11 November 1911, they were top of the First Division with Middlesbrough one point behind them in second place. A record crowd of 32,986 packed into the ground to see the clubs draw 1–1 with George Elliott scoring for 'Boro.

During the First World War, 'Boro won the Northern Victory League and completed the 'double' over Newcastle, winning 3–0 at home and 1–0 at St James Park.

'Boro's biggest win in the meeting with the Tyneside club came on 14 February 1931 when, after winning 3–1 at Ayresome Park, they travelled to St James Park and won 5–0 with goals from Camsell (2), Cameron, McKay and Warren. Two seasons later they suffered their heaviest defeat in this fixture when they lost 5–1 to the Magpies at St James Park.

In the first five home league meetings after the Second World War, Middlesbrough won them all and completed the 'double' in seasons 1949–50 and 1951–52. In 1953–54, both clubs won the away fixture, Newcastle 3–2 at Ayresome Park on Christmas Day and 'Boro by the same scoreline at St James Park on Boxing Day! Due to various promotions and relegations, the clubs only met in seasons 1963–64 and 1964–65 over the next twenty years.

When 'Boro entertained the Magpies on the final day of the 1989–90 season, they had to win and hope that Leeds won at Bournemouth to retain their place in the Second Division. Leeds won at Dean Court and 'Boro thrashed Newcastle 4–1 with Bernie Slaven and Ian Baird scoring two goals apiece.

The clubs last met on 2 May 2000 when goals from Festa and Juninho gave 'Boro a 2-2 draw at the Cellnet Stadium.

Middlesbrough's record against Newcastle United in the various competitions is as follows:

	P	W	D	L	F	A
Football League	92	29	28	35	111	125
FA Cup	4	2	0	2	7	9
Football League Cup	5	2	1	2	6	5
Anglo-Scottish Cup	2	0	1	1	2	5
Texaco Cup	1	0	0	1	0	4
TOTAL	104	33	30	41	126	148

NICKNAMES

Middlesbrough are known as 'Boro or Ironsides (in reference to the area's heavy industries). Many players in the club's history have been fondly known by their nicknames, including:

Jimmy Watson	1907–1910	'Daddy Long Legs'
Walter Holmes	1914–1928	'Squire'
Craig Johnston	1978–1981	'Roo'
Bernie Slaven	1985–1993	'The Wolfman'

NON-LEAGUE

During their first season as a Football League club, Middlesbrough lost their first FA Cup match against non-League opposition when they went down 2–1 at home to Jarrow. In 1996–97 the last time 'Boro faced non-League opposition in the FA Cup they beat Hednesford Town 3–2 on their way to the final where they lost 2–0 to Chelsea.

The club's full record against non-League opposition in the FA Cup since their acceptance to the Football League is as follows:

Date	Opposition	Stage	Venue	Score
28.10.1899	Jarrow	Q1	Home	1–2
03.11.1900	Willington Athletic	Q1	Home	3–3
07.11.1900	Willington Athletic	Q1(R)	Away	0–0
12.11.1900	Willington Athletic	Q1(2R)	Home	8–0
17.11.1900	Jarrow	Q2	Home	3–0
08.12.1900	Bishop Auckland	Q3	Home	4–0
23.02.1901	Kettering Town	Rd 3	Home	5–0
25.01.1902	Bristol Rovers	Rd 1	Home	1–1
29.01.1902	Bristol Rovers	Rd 1(R)	Away	0–1
06.02.1904	Millwall	Rd 1	Away	2–0
04.02.1905	Tottenham Hotspur	Rd 1	Home	1–1

08.02.1905	Tottenham Hotspur	Rd 1(R)	Away	0–1
03.02.1906	Brighton & H.A.	Rd 2	Away	1–1
07.02.1906	Brighton & H.A.	Rd 2(R)	Home	1–1
12.02.1906	Brighton & H.A.	Rd 2(2R)	Neutral*	3–1
24.02.1906	Southampton	Rd 3	Away	1–6
12.01.1907	Northampton Town	Rd 1	Home	4–2
02.02.1907	Brentford	Rd 2	Away	0–1
03.02.1912	West Ham United	Rd 2	Home	1–1
08.02.1912	West Ham United	Rd 2(R)	Away	1–2
11.01.1913	Millwall	Rd 1	Away	0–0
15.01.1913	Millwall	Rd 1(R)	Home	4–1
01.02.1913	Queen's Park.R	Rd 2	Home	3–2
09.01.1915	Goole Town	Rd 1	Home	9–3
04.01.1975	Wycombe Wanderers	Rd 3	Away	0–0
07.01.1975	Wycombe Wanderers	Rd 3(R)	Home	1–0
08.01.1983	Bishop's Stortford	Rd 3	Home	2–2
11.01.1983	Bishop's Stortford	Rd 3(R)	Away	2–1
09.01.1988	Sutton United	Rd 3	Away	1–1
12.01.1988	Sutton United	Rd 3(R)	Home	1–0
25.01.1997	Hednesford Town	Rd 4	Away	3–2

* Played at Bramall Lane.

NORTHERN LEAGUE

Middlesbrough were one of the ten founder members of the Northern League and played their first game in the competition at home to Elswick Rangers on 14 September 1889. The most successful team in the early years of the Northern League were Middlesbrough Ironopolis who won three consecutive Championships. 'Boro were runners-up in 1890–91 and 1891–92, though following Ironopolis' acceptance into the Football League, Middlesbrough went on to win the Northern League Championship in 1893–94, 1894–95 and 1896–97 before they themselves were accepted into the Football League in May 1899.

NURSE, MEL

Welsh schoolboy centre-half Mel Nurse began his league career with his home-town club, Swansea City, signing professional forms for the Vetch Field club in June 1955. Over the next seven seasons, Nurse gave many outstanding performances at the heart of the Swansea defence and in 1960 after winning two Welsh Under-23 caps, he made his full international

debut against England at Wembley. It was the first of 12 full caps for his country, nine of them won whilst with the Swans.

He proved himself to be an inspirational leader, captaining the Swans during his last few seasons with the club. However, as the Welsh club struggled in the lower reaches of the Second Division, Nurse requested a transfer on a number of occasions, all of which were turned down.

Eventually though, the Swans had to release him and in September 1962 he joined Middlesbrough for a fee of £25,000.

His first game in 'Boro's colours came in a 4–3 win at Grimsby Town and it wasn't long before his performances led to him being appointed club captain. Over the next three seasons, Nurse was a virtual ever-present and though he only scored nine goals in 124 games for the Teeside club, many were spectacular efforts. One of his strikes whilst a 'Boro player was against his former club and sent them spiralling into the Third Division. In the summer of 1965, Nurse joined Swindon Town and spent three seasons at the County Ground before returning to Swansea in June 1968.

He scored 11 goals in 256 League games in his two spells with the club before entering non-League football with Suffolk club, Bury. He later ended his career with Merthyr Tydfil, for whom he was playing when he suffered a broken leg.

O

OLDEST PLAYER

The oldest player to line up in a Middlesbrough team is Bryan Robson. He was 39 years 355 days old when he played his last game for the club against Arsenal (Away 0–2) on New Year's Day 1997.

O'ROURKE, JOHN

After playing as an amateur with both Arsenal and Chelsea, Northampton-born striker John O'Rourke joined Luton Town. At Kenilworth Road he proved to be a prolific marksman, netting 64 goals in 84 games. It was this scoring ratio that prompted Middlesbrough boss Stan Anderson to sign O'Rourke for the Ayresome Park club.

He scored two goals on his debut as 'Boro won 3–2 at Colchester United on the opening day of the 1966–67 season. Forming a formidable striking partnership with Arthur Horsfield, O'Rourke scored 30 goals in 43 games to help 'Boro win promotion to the Second Division. His total included hat-tricks in the league victories over Swindon Town (Home 4–0) and Oxford United (Home 4–1) as well as three of the club's goals in a 5–2 League Cup win at Chester City.

At the end of the season, O'Rourke won international recognition when he was selected for the England Under-23 side against Turkey in Ankara and where not surprisingly, he scored one of England's goals.

In 1967–68, O'Rourke initially struggled to find his shooting boots but as the season unfolded, he found the net 11 times in the space of

25 games including hat-tricks against Derby County (Away 4–2) and Carlisle United (Home 4–0). O'Rourke had scored 42 goals in 72 games for 'Boro when Ipswich Town manager Bobby Robson took him to Portman Road and First Division football. His stay in Suffolk was brief and he moved to Coventry City before later playing for Queen's Park Rangers and Bournemouth.

ORRITT, BRYAN

One of the few Welsh-speaking players in the Football League, Bryan Orritt was playing for Bangor in the Cheshire League at the age of 17 and was twice chosen as the reserve for the Welsh international youth team. He turned professional with Birmingham City in January 1956, making his league debut in a 1–1 draw at Leeds United in October 1956.

Though he was able to play in a variety of positions, he found it difficult to hold down a regular place in the 'Boro side. His best season for the club was 1957–58 when he netted 12 goals in 27 games. He played for Birmingham in the 1960 and 1961 Inter Cities Fairs Cup Finals and won three Welsh Under-23 caps. Having scored 27 goals in 119 games, Orritt was transferred to Middlesbrough in March 1962 while serving a seven-day suspension following an incident during his time at St Andrew's.

He made his debut in a 3–2 home win over Charlton Athletic and went on to be a virtual ever-present for the next four seasons. One of the club's greatest-ever utility players, he appeared in all 11 positions for 'Boro and was their first playing substitute when he replaced Neville Chapman at Preston North End in September 1965. He had scored 23 goals in 128 games when he left the League scene and emigrated to South Africa to play for Johannesburg.

OTTO, HEINE

Dutchman Heine Otto began his career with Twente Enschede, replacing international Arnold Muhren who had left to join Ipswich Town. After a number of impressive performances for the Dutch Under-23 side, he was given his full international debut for the match against Yugoslavia but only played for the last 20 minutes of the match.

In the summer of 1981, Otto followed Muhren to England to sign for Middlesbrough, making a goalscoring debut in a 3–1 home defeat by Tottenham Hotspur on the opening day of the 1981–82 season. Though the

club made early exits in both cup competitions and finished bottom of the First Division, Otto was the club's leading scorer with five goals!

A versatile player with the ability to score goals, he appeared in six different numbered shirts during his four seasons at Ayresome Park.

He had scored 28 goals in 187 games for 'Boro when he turned down the chance of an extension to his contract and returned to Holland to continue his career with Den Haag in the Dutch Second Division. There he established a Dutch record for the most consecutive appearances before hanging up his boots to become coach with Ajax.

OVERSEAS PLAYERS

One of the club's first overseas players was Bosco Jankovic, a Yugoslavian international who arrived at Ayresome Park from Zeljeznicar in February 1979. Able to play in any of the forward positions, he scored 18 goals in 62 games before returning to his homeland after three seasons with 'Boro.

Heine Otto joined Middlesbrough from Dutch team Twente Enschede. The winner of one full cap, he also played a number of times for Holland's Under-23 side. After scoring on his debut in a 3–1 defeat by Spurs, he went on to score 28 goals in 187 games before moving to Dutch Second Division club, Den Haag.

Having represented Bolivia in the 1994 World Cup Finals, Jamie Moreno joined 'Boro in September of that year and though he adapted well to the way the game is played in the Football League, he only made 29 appearances for the club over two seasons.

Uwe Fuchs spent a short spell on loan with Middlesbrough midway through the 1994–95 season. The Kaiserslautern striker scored nine goals in 15 games including a hat-trick in a 3–0 win over Bristol City.

Jan Aage Fjortoft joined Middlesbrough from Swindon Town for £1.3 million in March 1995. The Norwegian international was the club's record signing when he arrived at Ayresome Park and soon won over the fans with his wholehearted displays.

Brazilian Juninho joined 'Boro from Sao Paulo for £4.75 million. He endeared himself to football fans up and down the country, not only with his deceptive body swerve and unbelievable stamina but also with his genuine sportsmanship which was refreshing to say the least. He went on to score 17 goals in 74 games before leaving to play for Atletico Madrid who paid £12 million for his services. Juninho returned to Middlesbrough on loan in September 1999.

The brilliant Brazilian Emerson arrived on Teeside from Porto for £4 million. Despite many outstanding performances, his relationship with the 'Boro fans was one that tested their patience following his absences from the club in 1996–97. He went on to score 11 goals in 70 games before leaving to play for Tenerife.

Fabrizio Ravanelli, alias 'The White Feather' joined 'Boro from Juventus for a club record fee of £7 million. He scored a hat-trick on his debut as Middlesbrough drew 3–3 with Liverpool and went on to score 31 League and Cup goals in his first season on Teeside, helping the club reach both the FA and League Cup Finals. After the club had been relegated, the Italian international left to play for Marseilles who splashed out £5.3 million for the then 29–year-old.

Danish international centre-forward Mikkel Beck joined 'Boro from Fortuna Cologne following a legal wrangle with the German Second Division club. A brilliant opportunist striker, he went on to score 31 goals in 115 games before being transferred to Derby County for £500,000 in March 1999.

Gianluca Festa first appeared on Teeside when playing for Inter Milan in a friendly in August 1996. The vastly experienced defender soon settled in the north-east after joining 'Boro from the Italian giants in January 1997 for £2.7 million. Most popular with the Middlesbrough fans, the hard-tackling Festa has now appeared in 96 games. Vladimir Kinder arrived on the same day as Festa for a fee of £1 million from Slovan Bratislava. Sent-off during the FA Cup semi-final clash against Second Division Chesterfield, Kinder has now appeared in 49 games for 'Boro.

Marco Branca signed for Middlesbrough from Inter Milan for £1 million in February 1998 and set Teeside alight with his goalscoring feats. He netted 10 goals in his first 12 games for the club including a hat-trick in a 4–0 win over Bury. The 1998–99 season saw him struggle with a mystery injury and his future at the Riverside Stadium may be uncertain.

Columbian international Hamilton Ricard arrived at Middlesbrough in March 1998 for a fee of £3 million. The former Deportivo player had an outstanding 1998–99 season, scoring 18 goals in 40 League and Cup games despite many feeling that he has yet to reach his peak, having now taken his tally of goals to 34 in 90 games.

OWN GOALS

Bobby Stuart was certainly not the most popular man at Ayresome Park in 1934–35 after breaking the record for own goals in a season, when

he scored five times against his own team!

George Hardwick put through his own goal on his debut for Middlesbrough against Bolton Wanderers on 18 December 1937 after less than a minute!

Another 'Boro favourite to put through his own goal was 'keeper Tim Williamson who punched the ball into his own net on his international debut for England against Ireland at Ayresome Park on 25 February 1905!

P

PALLISTER, GARY

Gary Pallister began his career with Billingham Town in the Northern League and though he went to Ayresome Park for a trial when Malcolm Allison was manager, he was released after just one Central League appearance. Allison's successor Willie Maddren had kept an eye on the centre-half's progress and just over a year later, the Ramsgate-born defender signed for 'Boro.

He made his debut in a 3–0 defeat at Wimbledon on the opening day of the 1985–86 season but then didn't play again until November, spending much of that time on loan with Darlington. On his return he formed an outstanding defensive partnership with Tony Mowbray and became the first player from the Second Division to be selected by Bobby Robson for the full England squad but 'Boro manager Bruce Rioch had to pull him out of the party to play for the club in the end of season play-offs. Pallister eventually won the first of 22 full caps for England against Hungary in 1988.

When 'Boro were relegated at the end of the 1988–89 season, Pallister left Ayresome Park and joined Manchester United for £2.3 million. The towering 6ft 4ins defender did not always look comfortable in his first season at Old Trafford but as time progressed, he began to look more confident and by 1992 was impressing his colleagues enough to be named PFA Player of the Year.

Pallister helped United to win their first League Championship since

1967 when they won the Premier League title in 1992–93. Since then he has won a further three Championship medals, three FA Cup winners' medals, a League Cup winners' medal and a European Cup Winners' Cup medal. He went on to appear in 437 games for United before rejoining Middlesbrough in the summer of 1998.

A towering presence in the air, Pallister has now taken his total of first team appearances in his two spells with the club to 242..

Gary Pallister

PARKINSON, GARY

After a short apprenticeship with Everton was terminated because of home sickness, the young Parkinson continued his career nearer to home with Middlesbrough before signing as a professional in January 1986. He made his debut for 'Boro in the 2–2 home draw against Port Vale at Hartlepool's Victoria Ground on the opening day of the 1986–87 season and went on to be one of five ever-presents as the club won promotion from the Third Division as runners-up to Bournemouth.

He was still a regular the following season as 'Boro stormed straight through the Second Division to the First via a two-legged play-off victory over Chelsea. It was at the end of that campaign that he was switched from the centre of defence where he partnered Gary Pallister to right-back. He went on to play in 258 League and Cup games before following a loan spell with Southend United, he joined Bolton Wanderers.

Things never worked out for him at Burnden Park and in January 1994 he moved to Burnley. An automatic choice for the rest of that campaign, he scored the winning goal at Wembley as the Clarets beat Stockport County in the play-off final to win promotion to the new First Division. He left Turf Moor in the summer of 1997 to join Preston North End where during the course of the 1998–99 season, he played his 500th senior game.

PEACOCK, ALAN

Though he signed professional forms for his home-town club in November 1954, Alan Peacock had to wait a year before making his Middlesbrough debut in a 7–2 defeat at Bristol Rovers! He appeared in just six games in that 1955–56 season, his two goals coming in a 4–2 win over Nottingham Forest.

However, it was 1957–58 before he established a regular place in the 'Boro side, his total of 15 goals in 22 games including a hat-trick in a 4–1 home win over Cardiff City. Forming a lethal striking partnership with Brian Clough, Alan Peacock scored 19 goals in 1958–59 including another hat-trick in the 6–1 defeat of Scunthorpe United. The following season, Peacock scored four of 'Boro's goals in a 7–1 win at the Baseball Ground as Derby County were completely overrun.

Once Clough had left Ayresome Park to join Sunderland, Peacock came into his own and in 1961–62 top-scored with 24 goals in 34 games including four in a 5–1 home win over Rotherham United. Also that season he netted eight goals in cup competitions including a hat-trick in a 6–3 win at Tranmere Rovers. His form that season earned him a place in the England squad for the 1962 World Cup Finals in Chile and he went on to win six caps. Peacock's best season for 'Boro in terms of goals scored was 1962–63 when he netted 31 in 40 games including his sixth hat-trick for the club in a 4–3 win at Charlton Athletic. Peacock had scored 141 goals in 238 games for 'Boro when in February 1964 he joined Leeds United for £55,000.

At Elland Road he won a Second Division Championship medal and appeared in the 1965 FA Cup Final against Liverpool but after scoring 31 goals in 65 games he left to join Plymouth Argyle. Within a matter of months of signing for the Home Park club, Peacock was forced to retire following a knee injury.

PEARS, STEPHEN

Stephen Pears was spotted playing junior football by Manchester United and after a short-apprenticeship at Old Trafford, he was taken on as a full-time professional in 1979. Sadly for Pears he could not break into the United side and spent the next six seasons as a permanent reserve before getting four First Division calls in 1984–85, a season after he had made 12 league appearances on loan at Middlesbrough.

The first of these appearances had been in a 2–0 win over Cardiff City. His form in that loan spell was such that an appeal was made to try and raise the £80,000 needed to make the move permanent. The target wasn't reached and Pears returned to Old Trafford.

'Boro manager Willie Maddren finally moved in to secure his full transfer in the summer of 1985, paying United a six-figure fee for his services. He was installed as first-choice 'keeper at Ayresome Park at the start of the 1985–86 campaign and after that missed very few games over the next nine seasons.

Injuries plagued him occasionally but he was in outstanding form in 1987–88 as 'Boro won promotion from the Second Division via the play-offs. During the club's promotion-challenging season of 1991–92, Pears was involved in some of Graham Taylor's England squads but was sadly forced to withdraw after fracturing a cheekbone. Pears played in 424 games for 'Boro before being released at the end of the 1994–95 season and joining Liverpool.

He later played for Hartlepool United where he ended his league career.

PEARSON, NIGEL

Nigel Pearson was playing non-League football for Heanor Town when Shrewsbury Town paid £5,000 to take him to Gay Meadow in November 1981. He had to wait nine months before making his League debut at Oldham Athletic but after having won a regular place in the side, was badly injured and out of action for over a year. He made a good recovery and was ever-present during the 1986–87 season. The central defender had

made 181 first team appearances for Shrewsbury before signing for Sheffield Wednesday for £250,000 in November 1987.

In his first few seasons at Hillsborough, he hardly missed a game. Inspiring by example, he led the Owls to promotion from the Second Division and victory in the League Cup Final in 1990–91, scoring 12 goals, notably from free-kicks and corners. Frequently rested or absent through injury, he broke a leg in the 1992–93 League Cup semi-final at Blackburn. At the end of the following season after appearing in 224 games for the Owls, he joined Middlesbrough for £500,000.

Brave in the air and uncompromising on the ground, Pearson made his 'Boro debut in a 2–0 home win over Burnley on the opening day of the 1994–95 season. In his first season with the club, Pearson scored three goals in 33 games to help 'Boro win the First Division Championship, his first helping them secure a point in a 2–2 draw against Sunderland.

Bryan Robson soon appointed Pearson as the club's captain and it wasn't long before Middlesbrough supporters named him 'Captain Fantastic', as he had an inspirational effect on the team. Over the next five seasons, Pearson was a model of consistency, leading the club to both the FA Cup and League Cup Finals in 1996–97. The following season was Pearson's last as a player and after scoring five goals in 139 games, he led 'Boro back to the Premier League at the first attempt, his performances earning him selection for the award-winning PFA First Division select.

PEASE, BILLY

Billy Pease began his career with his home-town club, Leeds City but when the club were expelled from the Football League in October 1919, he left to join Northampton Town who had just gained acceptance to the newly formed Third Division (South).

After turning in a series of outstanding performances for the Cobblers over the next few seasons, the goalscoring winger was signed by Middlesbrough in May 1926 for £2,000. After making his debut in a 3–0 defeat at Chelsea on the opening day of the 1926–27 season, he went on to score 23 goals in 30 games to help 'Boro win the Second Division Championship. Though Middlesbrough were relegated the following season, Pease still found the net with great regularity and scored his first hat-trick for the club in a 4–1 win at Bury. In 1928–29 when 'Boro won the Second Division title again, Pease was in tremendous form, scoring 27

goals in 35 games including four in the 8–3 defeat of Wolves and a hat-trick in the 3–1 win over Notts County.

Capped against Wales in February 1927, Pease went on to score 102 goals in 238 games for Middlesbrough before leaving Ayresome Park in the summer of 1933 to join Luton Town where he ended his playing career.

PENALTIES

The club's first penalty in the Football League was scored by John Brown in the 3–2 win at Chesterfield on 22 September 1900.

'Boro's long-serving goalkeeper Tim Williamson, who appeared in 602 games, netted twice from the penalty-spot, in the 2–2 draw against Liverpool in April 1910 and in the 3–0 home win over Bristol City in September 1910.

In 1962–63, 'Boro winger Arthur Kaye scored 10 penalties. The player who has scored most League and Cup penalties for the club is John Hickton with 29 followed by Bill Harris with 25 and George Elliott with 19.

PENTLAND, FRED

After beginning his Football League career with Small Heath in August 1900, he joined Blackpool before returning to First Division football with Blackburn Rovers towards the end of 1903. After a short spell with Brentford, he moved to Queen's Park Rangers from where Middlesbrough signed him towards the end of the 1907–08 season.

Pentland won the first of five full caps for England whilst with Middlesbrough when he played against Wales in March 1909, having made his first team debut in a 1–0 home win over Bradford City on the opening day of the 1908–09 season. Pentland scored 11 goals in 95 League and Cup games for 'Boro before joining Halifax and later playing for Stoke.

When the First World War broke out, Fred Pentland was coaching in Germany and was interned for the duration along with Steve Bloomer.

After the hostilities were over, he coached in France for a short while before spending 15 years in Spain coaching Atletico Bilbao until the outbreak of the Civil War in 1936.

When he returned to England he coached Brentford before managing Barrow for a brief spell.

PHILLIPS, JIMMY

After working his way up through Bolton Wanderers' junior and reserve

teams, Jimmy Phillips made his first team debut as a substitute in a 1–0 home defeat by Gillingham in April 1984. Following Ray Deakin's departure to Burnley, Phillips established himself as the club's first-choice left-back but in March 1987, Glasgow Rangers paid £75,000 to take young Phillips to Ibrox Park and the following season he played in four European Cup ties for the Scottish champions. In the summer of 1988 he joined Oxford United for £110,000 before signing for Middlesbrough who were then managed by Colin Todd.

He made his 'Boro debut in a 3–0 home defeat by Blackburn Rovers in March 1990 and proceeded to miss very few games over the next three seasons, helping the club win promotion to the Premier League in 1991–92. After just one season in the top flight, Phillips, who had scored eight goals in 170 games rejoined the Wanderers for a fee of £300,000.

He was ever-present in 1994–95 when the club won promotion to the Premiership and reached the League Cup Final. He won a First Division Championship medal in 1996–97 and has now taken his total of first team appearances in two spells with his home-town club, in which he has scored nine goals to over 400.

Jimmy Phillips

PITCH

The Riverside Stadium pitch measures 115 yards by 74 yards.

PLASTIC

Four Football League clubs replaced their normal grass playing pitches with artificial surfaces at one stage or another. Queen's Park Rangers were the first in 1981 but the Loftus Road artificial pitch was discarded in 1988 in favour of a return to turf. Oldham Athletic, Luton Town and Preston North End are the other three clubs.

'Boro never played on the Deepdale plastic and lost 1–0 on Luton's Kenilworth Road plastic on their only visit in 1988–89.

The club's three visits to Oldham Athletic's Boundary Park plastic all resulted in defeats and though 'Boro drew 1–1 on their first visit to Queen's Park Rangers' Loftus Road plastic in an FA Cup tie in 1981–82, their next visit resulted in their heaviest-ever defeat on plastic when they lost 6–1.

PLATT, JIM

Northern Ireland international goalkeeper Jim Platt began his career with Ballymena. His form for the Irish club led to Liverpool offering him a trial but they had just signed Ray Clemence from Scunthorpe United and decided not to offer Platt terms. He returned to Ballymena where he won Irish Amateur caps and an Irish FA Cup runners-up medal before joining Middlesbrough for a fee of £7,000 in the summer of 1970.

It was October 1971 before he displaced 'Boro's first-choice 'keeper Willie Whigham in a 1–0 home win over Blackpool, after which he missed very few games between the posts in 12 seasons at Ayresome Park. At the end of his first season with the club he was voted 'Boro's Player of the Year. When Middlesbrough won the Second Division Championship in 1973–74, Platt was in tremendous form, conceding just 28 goals in 40 appearances. His form led to him winning full international honours for Northern Ireland, his first cap coming against Israel in March 1974.

Midway through the 1978–79 season, Platt found himself out of favour following a well-publicised row with manager Jack Charlton over tactics. He was loaned out to Hartlepool and Cardiff City but returned to Ayresome Park to win back his first team place. In 1980–81 he was voted the north-east's Player of the Year and at the end of the season was awarded a testimonial game against Sunderland. Platt appeared in

one game during Northern Ireland's 1982 World Cup Finals exploits, taking his total of caps while playing for Middlesbrough to 20. He had appeared in 481 games for 'Boro when he returned to Ireland to become player-manager of Ballymena.

On returning to the north-east he had a spell as assistant-manager to David Hodgson at Darlington, replacing him as manager when he left. However, early in the 1996–97 season, he too was dismissed but he wasn't out of the game for long, taking over the reins at Gateshead.

Jim Platt

PLAY-OFFS

In 1987–88, Middlesbrough needed to beat Leicester City at Ayresome Park in the last game of the season to win promotion to the First Division. They lost 2–1 and had to settle for a place in the play-offs. Their opponents in the two-legged semi-final were Bradford City. The first match at Valley Parade saw the home side take the lead through Goddard and though Trevor Senior equalised for 'Boro two minutes later, Stuart McCall restored City's lead within a matter of seconds.

The second leg at Ayresome Park three days later saw Bernie Slaven

level the scores on aggregate and as there was no further scoring over the 90 minutes, the game went into extra-Time. Within the first minute, a goal by Gary Hamilton secured 'Boro's place in the final. Chelsea were Middlesbrough's opponents but the London club were beaten 2–0 with Trevor Senior and Bernie Slaven the 'Boro scorers. In the second leg at Stamford Bridge, Gordon Durie pulled a goal back after 19 minutes but 'Boro's defence stood firm and there was no further scoring. Middlesbrough had won promotion to the First Division.

The club experienced the play-offs a second time in 1990–91. After finishing seventh in Division Two, 'Boro met Notts County in the two-legged semi-final. They found the Meadow Lane club tough opposition and after only managing a 1–1 draw in the first match at Ayresome Park, lost to the only goal of the game in the return leg.

POINTS

Under the three points for a win system which was introduced in 1981–82, Middlesbrough's best points tally was 94 in 1986–87 when the club were runners-up in the Third Division. However, the club's best points haul under the old two points for a win system was 65 in 1973–74 when they won the Second Division Championship. Middlesbrough's worst record under either system was the meagre 22 points secured in 1922–23 when the club finished bottom of the First Division and were relegated.

POLLOCK, JAMIE

One of the club's brightest homegrown talents of recent years, the central midfielder made his Middlesbrough debut as a substitute for Paul Wilkinson in a 4–1 home win over Leeds United in August 1992. His consistency earned him international recognition for England at Under-21 level and over four seasons with the club, he scored 19 goals in 193 games, winning a First Division Championship medal in 1994–95.

In the summer of 1996, Pollock left 'Boro on a free transfer to play for Osasuna in the Spanish Second Division. It was an unhappy move and he jumped at the chance to return to the Football League with Bolton Wanderers in November 1996. Colin Todd's £1.5 million signing helped the Trotters win the First Division title, as he scored in four consecutive games at the end of the season, including the club's 100th league goal. Despite being played on the right of midfield, rather than in his preferred central position, Pollock continued to be a real crowd pleaser, scoring eight goals in 55 games before being allowed to join

Manchester City for £1 million as they tried to avoid relegation to the Second Division.

Appointed club captain, he couldn't prevent City's relegation but helped them win promotion via the play-offs in 1998–99 despite missing much of the first half of the season due to a hernia. He was also a member of the City side that won promotion to the Premier League in 1999-2000.

POSTPONED

The bleak winter of 1962–63, described at the time as the modern ice-age, proved to be one of the most chaotic seasons in British soccer history. The worst Saturday for league action in that awful winter was 9 February when only seven Football League fixtures went ahead and the entire Scottish League programme was frozen off. Middlesbrough did play on 9 February, winning an exciting game at Plymouth Argyle 5–4. The worst Saturday for the FA Cup was 5 January, the day of the third round when only three of the 32 ties could be played. 'Boro didn't play one single game in the month of January and their tie against Blackburn Rovers was the last tie to be settled. It was postponed 10 times but when the two teams did meet on 5 March, the game at Ewood Park ended all-square at 1–1. The replay at Ayresome Park six days later saw 'Boro win 3–1 with two goals from Alan Peacock and a penalty by Arthur Kaye.

PREMIER LEAGUE

During the first season of Premier League football, 1992–93, Middlesbrough suffered a number of heavy defeats on their travels - Aston Villa (1–5), Chelsea (0–4), Crystal Palace (1–4), Liverpool (1–4), and Oldham Athletic (1–4) - to end the season in 21st place and so were relegated to the First Division. After finishing ninth in Division One in 1993–94, 'Boro returned to the Premier League as First Division Champions the following season with new player-manager Bryan Robson leading the way. During the close season the club moved to a brand new 31,000 all-seater stadium - the Cellnet Riverside Stadium, situated in the harbourside redevelopment area.

In 1995–96, 'Boro made a solid start to the season and in October after five consecutive victories, including four clean sheets, moved into fourth place. Robson who had already spent £5.25 million on Nick Barmby, paid £4.75 million on the Brazilian Player of the Year, Juninho from Sao Paulo.

Despite these signings, 'Boro suffered eight successive Premiership

defeats after the turn of the year, to equal the worst run in the club's history. Results did pick up towards the end of the campaign and 'Boro ended the season in 12th place. There had been a distinct lack of goals in 1995–96 and so Robson paid £7 million for the services of Italian international striker Fabrizio Ravanelli.

Other overseas players to join 'Boro's cause were the Brazilian Emerson and Mikkel Beck of Fortuna Cologne. Ravanelli marked his debut in English football with a hat-trick in a 3–3 draw with Liverpool but despite his and Juninho's determination to keep the club in the Premiership, a run of defeats took 'Boro to the foot of the table. Though they moved out of the bottom three, four games without a win meant they had to win at Leeds on the final day. They could only manage a 1–1 draw and so the Riverside club became the most expensively assembled squad to fall from the Premiership.

Both Juninho and Ravanelli left the club as Robson over the course of the 1997–98 season brought in Merson, Townsend and Gascoigne to help the club win promotion back to the Premier League as runners-up to Nottingham Forest.

'Boro made a good start to the 1998–99 Premier League season, losing just two of their opening 18 fixtures and after beating Manchester United 3–2 at Old Trafford, occupied fourth place in the table. The club then went nine matches without a win, scoring just once in a spell of six games. Though they then embarked on a seven match unbeaten run, they were brought down to earth by Arsenal who won 6–1 at the Riverside Stadium. The club ended the season in ninth place with Columbian Hamilton Ricard top-scoring with 15 goals.

PROCTOR, MARK

Middlesbrough-born Mark Proctor had a trial with Leeds United when he was 14 but returned to Teeside homesick after only a few days with the Elland Road club and signed associate schoolboy forms for Middlesbrough. Before becoming a full-time professional, Proctor captained the England Youth side in the international tournament in Las Palmas.

He made his 'Boro debut in a 3–1 win at Birmingham City in the second game of the 1978–79 season after which he was a virtual ever-present for the next three campaigns. He went on to score 14 goals from 135 appearances before his impressive performances in midfield led to Nottingham Forest paying £440,000 for his services in the summer of 1981. Whilst at Ayresome Park, Proctor won two caps for England at Under-21

level and played in a similar total whilst with Forest. Unable to settle at the City Ground, he was loaned to Sunderland before eventually signing for the Wearsiders on a permanent basis. He went on to score 23 goals in 139 League and Cup games for Sunderland before Sheffield Wednesday paid £275,000 to take him to Hillsborough in September 1987.

In March 1989, Proctor made a surprise return to Ayresome Park, costing Bruce Rioch £300,000. Though he failed to save the club from relegation, he helped them to the play-offs in 1991 and to promotion the following season, taking his tally of goals to 20 in 273 appearances in his two spells. He later had a loan spell with Tranmere Rovers before retiring to work on Teeside with the Football Academy.

PROMOTION

Middlesbrough have been promoted on ten occasions. The first occasion was in 1901–02 when the club finished runners-up to West Bromwich Albion in the Second Division. After 18 seasons of top flight football, 'Boro were relegated in 1923–24 but won promotion as Second Division champions in 1926–27. Sadly their stay in the First Division lasted just one season but the club were promoted immediately after winning the Second Division title again in 1928–29.

After another spell of 18 seasons in the First Division, 'Boro were relegated to the Second Division and in 1965–66 fell into the Third Division for the first time in their history. Despite finishing 12 points behind champions Queen's Park Rangers, 'Boro won promotion at the first attempt as they ended the campaign one point ahead of third-placed Watford. In 1973–74, 'Boro were promoted for the fifth time in their history after ending the season as Second Division champions. Relegation to Division Two followed in 1981–82 after eight seasons of First Division football before in 1985–86 the club entered the Third Division again. As in their previous season in Division Three, the club were promoted at the first attempt, finishing the campaign as runners-up to Bournemouth. 'Boro won promotion again the following season, finishing third in Division Two behind champions Millwall and runners-up Aston Villa. Relegated in 1988–89, 'Boro returned to the top flight in 1991–92 as runners-up to Ipswich Town but were relegated from the newly-formed Premier League after one season. The club bounced back in 1994–95 as First Division champions, finishing three points ahead of Reading. Following two seasons in the Premiership, 'Boro were relegated in 1996–97 but won promotion for a tenth time the following season as runners-up to Nottingham Forest.

Q

QUICKEST GOAL

Because the club's records do not include precise goal times, it is impossible to state accurately the club's quickest goalscorer. One that must be in contention occurred on 5 April 1999 when Columbian international Hamilton Rickard scored 'Boro's first goal well inside the first minute to help the Teeside club on their way to a 3–1 win over Wimbledon.

R

RAPID SCORING

On 18 November 1933, the season's lowest crowd of 6,461 saw the visitors Sheffield United take the lead after just three minutes when Baines' 25–yard shot entered the net off the underside of the crossbar. 'Boro drew level in the 22nd minute, courtesy of George Camsell, it being the start of seven goals being scored in a period of 23 minutes!

Ferguson, Camsell, Warren and Bruce netted to give 'Boro a 5–1 lead and though Pickering reduced the arrears for United, Bruce scored his second on the stroke of half-time to make the score 6–2 in Middlesbrough's favour.

Ten minutes after the restart, Camsell completed his hat-trick and Baxter extended 'Boro's lead before the Blades scored a third goal midway through the second-half. Bruce completed his hat-trick by scoring from the penalty-spot before Camsell netted his fourth to give 'Boro a 10–3 win!

RAVANELLI, FABRIZIO

Signed from Juventus for a club record £7 million, immediately prior to the 1996–97 campaign, Fabrizio Ravanelli did not make his debut in Italy's Serie A until he was 24–years-old. Ravanelli began is career with his home-town club, Perugia where his goalscoring exploits of a goal every other game led to his transfer to Avellino. Unable to settle at his new club, he had a loan spell at Casertana before moving to Reggiana.

In 1992 Juventus paid £3 million for Ravanelli's services. It proved to be money well spent, for in his last two seasons with the club, he helped them win the Serie A title and the European Champions League, scoring 53 goals in the process.

Nicknamed the 'White Feather', the Italian international made a sensational debut for 'Boro scoring a hat-trick in a 3–3 draw against Liverpool on the opening day of the 1996–97 season. Ravanelli, who celebrated each of his goals by lifting his shirt over his head, scored 31 League and Cup goals that season including four in the 7–0 League Cup win over Hereford United and a hat-trick in the 6–1 defeat of Derby County.

Following 'Boro's relegation to the First Division, Ravanelli, who had scored 32 goals in 50 games in his stay at the Riverside Stadium, left the club under a cloud in September 1997 to join Marseilles for £5.3 million.

RECEIPTS

The club's record receipts are £361,444 for the Coca Cola Cup semifinal second leg match against Liverpool at the Cellnet Riverside Stadium on 18 February 1998.

RELEGATION

Middlesbrough have suffered the experience of relegation on nine occasions. The first was in 1923–24 after 18 seasons of First Division football following their promotion in 1901–02. The club won just seven games and amassed only 22 points. After winning promotion in 1926–27, 'Boro were relegated the following season again after finishing bottom of the First Division. The club then spent another 18 seasons in the top flight after winning the Second Division Championship in 1928–29 before being relegated for a third time in 1953–54. The club suffered their fourth relegation in 1965–66 when they lost their Second Division status and had to play in the Third Division for the first time. After winning promotion at the first attempt, 'Boro won the Second Division Championship in 1973–74 and spent eight seasons playing First Division football before experiencing their sixth relegation in 1981–82. In 1985–86 the club were relegated to the Third Division again but as before, won promotion at the first attempt. A successive promotion took 'Boro into the First Division but in 1988–89 the club were relegated for a seventh time. After winning promotion to the newly-formed Premier League

in 1991–92, 'Boro lasted just one season, being relegated along with Crystal Palace and Nottingham Forest. They returned to the Premiership in 1994–95 but were relegated a ninth time in 1996–97 despite having the likes of Juninho and Ravanelli in their side.

RICKARD, HAMILTON

Columbian international Hamilton Rickard joined Middlesbrough from Deportivo Cali for £2 million in March 1998 and made his debut in the 3–0 win over Norwich City at the Riverside Stadium. He appeared in every game from his debut to the end of the season, though he was unable to produce the form most 'Boro fans expected of him. However, he was still in Columbia's World Cup 22 in France '98 and came off the bench to play against England in the group matches.

The 1998–99 season was a different story for the popular 'Ham the Man' who netted 18 League and Cup goals to become the club's leading goalscorer. In fact, whenever Rickard scored, 'Boro never lost a Premier League game!

Standing 6ft 2ins and weighing 14 stone, the strong Columbian is difficult to dislodge and his striking partnerships with both Brian Deane and towards the end of the season with Keith O'Neill are developing all the time. By the end of the 1999-2000 season, Rickard had scored 34 goals in 90 games, a total he seems likely to increase.

RIOCH, BRUCE

Scottish international wing-half Bruce Rioch played for Luton Town, Aston Villa, Derby County, Everton, Birmingham City, Sheffield United and Torquay United, where he gained his first experience of management.

However, his first success came following his appointment by Middlesbrough in February 1986. He guided the club from a dire financial position and lifted them from the Third to the First Division within two seasons. In 1986–87 he helped the club win promotion to the Second Division as runners-up to Bournemouth and in 1987–88 he took the club into the top flight via the play-offs. 'Boro were relegated in 1988–89 and in March 1990 with the club languishing near the foot of the Second Division, Rioch left Ayresome Park.

In less than a month he was in charge at Millwall and in 1990–91 took the London club to the Second Division play-offs but after their form slumped the following season, he resigned to later manage Bolton

Wanderers. He achieved promotion in his first season at Burnden Park as the Wanderers finished runners-up in Division Two. In 1993–94 he led Bolton to the sixth round of the FA Cup and the following season took the club to the League Cup Final and promotion to the Premiership via the play-offs.

In June 1995, Rioch left Bolton to manage Arsenal but after 15 months he was sacked and joined Queen's Park Rangers. He later managed Norwich City, but lost his job midway through the 1999-2000 season.

Bruce Rioch

RIPLEY, STUART

A member of the Middlesbrough Boys' team that shared the English Schools FA Trophy with Sunderland, Stuart Ripley joined the Ayresome Park club as an apprentice professional. He made his 'Boro debut as a substitute for Irving Nattrass in a 2–1 defeat at home to Oldham Athletic in February 1985. The following season he was loaned out to

145

Bolton Wanderers and scored on his debut for the Lancashire club in a 4–0 win over Newport County. It was 1986–87 before he established himself in the Middlesbrough side, helping the club win promotion from the Third Division. The following season he netted his first hat-trick for the club in a 6–0 home win over Sheffield United as 'Boro went into the top flight via the play-offs. Following 'Boro's relegation in 1988–89, many people thought Ripley would leave the club but he stayed loyal to the club and in 1991–92 helped them win promotion to the newly-formed Premier League.

Blackburn Rovers' manager Kenny Dalglish paid £1.3 million to take Ripley to Ewood Park. The winger had scored 32 goals in 312 games for

Stuart Ripley

Middlesbrough but had made many more for his colleagues with his accurate crossing of the ball.

He helped Rovers win the League Championship in 1994–95, his form helping him win the first of his two full caps for England when he played against San Marino. Ripley, who was often hampered by injuries during his six seasons at Ewood Park, scored 16 goals in 228 games before being transferred to Southampton for £1.5 million in the summer of 1998.

RIVERSIDE STADIUM

It was December 1993 when a joint venture was established between Middlesbrough Borough Council, Teeside Development Corporation and the football club to build a new stadium on the banks of the River Tees.

The site which was used for petro-chemical storage was cleared and decontaminated by the Teeside Development Corporation. They also prepared the stadium's foundations, provided access to the site and laid out the car parks. Middlesbrough Football Club had to provide the funds for all the above ground construction. This came to a total of £12 million of which £3 million came from the Football Trust. Another £4 million came from 'Cellnet' the mobile telephone company who signed a 10–year sponsorship deal with the club to have the prefix added to the stadium's name.

Though there were a number of delays the stadium was eventually opened on 26 August 1995 when the club played its first game at the Cellnet Riverside Stadium against Chelsea. For the record, a crowd of 28,286 saw 'Boro beat the Stamford Bridge club 2–0.

The ground's present capacity is 35,000 and at the time of writing, the club's record attendance at the Riverside Stadium is 34,800 for the visit of Leeds United on 26 February 2000.

ROBINSON, DICKIE

During the war, Dickie Robinson worked down the mines as a 'Bevin Boy' and 'guested' for nearby Dunfermline Athletic until April 1945 when he signed for Middlesbrough. When league football resumed in 1946–47, Robinson partnered George Hardwick at full-back and held his place in the side for the next 13 seasons. Although he never won full international honours, he represented the Football League and went on tour to South Africa with an FA party. Despite a series of niggling injuries, Robinson fought off all would be challengers for his position,

appearing in 416 League and Cup games in his time at Ayresome Park. His only goal for the club came in a 2–1 defeat at Doncaster Rovers on Boxing Day 1956 but it wasn't for the want of trying, for Robinson packed a powerful shot.

An excellent positional player and one of the fastest full-backs ever to play for the club, he left 'Boro in the summer of 1959 to join Barrow. He spent three seasons with the Holker Street club, appearing in 139 league games before hanging up his boots.

ROBSON, BRYAN

Bryan Robson's original football home is the north-east where as a teenager he would stand on the terraces of St James Park, Newcastle and shout on the Magpies.

He joined West Bromwich Albion in 1974 and they attempted to build him up in both physique and stature. His landlady would send him out at the start of the day with a mixture of raw egg, milk, sherry and sugar, followed by a night-cap of a bottle of Mackeson!

At the Hawthorns he played in several positions, this strategy helping him to understand many new things about the game. He best expressed his skills in midfield where he provided the ideal service for Regis and Cunningham. He suffered a great setback in the 1976–77 season when he broke his leg no fewer than three times! However, determination kept bringing him back and when Albion boss Ron Atkinson took charge at Manchester United, he returned to the Hawthorns and broke the trans-fer record by paying £1.5 million to take Robson to Old Trafford.

Initially a back-four player, he developed the attacking side of his game to such an extent that his powerful surges from midfield into the penalty area became his trademark. His midfield brilliance earned him a place in England's 1982 World Cup squad where he scored his country's first goal in the opening game against France after 27 seconds.

Bryan Robson took into the international game all the physical aggression needed to withstand the pressures of the English Football League, yet he also had a natural class that would impress in any of the World XI's of the past.

It is perhaps as a captain that Robson has made his greatest impres-sions, both for Manchester United and England. He led United to FA Cup Final victories and was their two-goal hero of the 1983 4–0 win over Brighton. He was the only England player to show his true form in the 1988 European Championships, though England's three consecutive

defeats were a great disappointment to him.

In 1991 he led United to victory over Barcelona in the European Cup Winners' Cup in Rotterdam and went on to score 100 goals in 465 games for the Red Devils before being appointed 'Boro's player-manager in May 1994.

Capped 90 times by England, he made his debut for Middlesbrough in a 2–0 home win over Burnley on the opening day of the 1994–95 season. In his first campaign with the club, he appeared in 22 games, helping to steer 'Boro into the Premier League at the first attempt.

After signing Juninho, Robson's first season in charge in the Premiership will be seen as one of consolidation as the club finished 12th, but in 1996–97 despite investing £7 million on Fabrizio Ravanelli, 'Boro finished 19th and were relegated. However, they did reach both the FA Cup and League Cup Finals, only to lose to Chelsea and Leicester City respectively.

Bryan Robson

In 1997–98, Robson inspired 'Boro to promotion at the first attempt and saw the club return to Wembley for a second successive League Cup Final but to another defeat at the hands of Chelsea.

ROBSON, JOHN

John Robson played in goal for Middlesbrough Swifts, the club's reserve side before becoming the club's secretary. When 'Boro reverted to amateur status, Robson became assistant-secretary to Albert Borrie. In 1899 following the club's acceptance into the Football League, Robson became the club's first manager. Within the space of three months he moulded 'Boro from a Northern League club into a side ready for Second Division football.

In 1901–02 he led the club to promotion to the First Division, 'Boro finishing runners-up to West Bromwich Albion. When there was an irregular payments scandal at the club in 1905, Robson was absolved of any responsibility in the episode but still vacated the post to take charge of Crystal Palace as the club's first manager. After a spell as Brighton's manager, in which the south coast club won the Southern League Championship in 1909–10, Robson became manager of Manchester United.

He later took over secretarial duties when J.J.Bentley resigned in 1916. Ill-health led to him stepping down to assistant in 1921 and shortly afterwards he died of pneumonia.

ROOKS, DICKY

A former Sunderland junior, he signed professional forms in June 1957 and sampled top flight soccer as Charlie Hurley's understudy before moving to Middlesbrough for £17,000 in August 1965. The natural successor to Welsh international centre-half Mel Nurse who had joined Swindon Town, Rooks made his debut in a disastrous 6–0 defeat at Huddersfield Town in the third game of the 1965–66 season. Towards the end of that campaign, which saw Middlesbrough relegated to the Third Division, Rooks played a few games at centre-forward and in one of these scored a hat-trick in a 5–3 defeat at Cardiff City. The following season he shared the centre-half duties with Bill Gates, helping the club win promotion at the first attempt. Rooks went on to score 14 goals in 150 games before Alan Dicks paid £17,000 to take him to Bristol City in the summer of 1969.

He helped the Ashton Gate club reach the League Cup semi-finals in

1970–71 and went on to score four times in 96 Second Division outings before joining Willington as player-coach. He later managed Scunthorpe United and coached in Zanzibar before becoming an FA Coach for Tyne and Wear linked with Sunderland's School of Excellence

ROWLEY, WALTER

Walter Rowley gave Bolton Wanderers 38 years' service as player, coach and manager. After playing his early football with local sides, the Little Hulton-born defender had a short spell with Oldham Athletic before signing for the Wanderers. He was Bolton's twelfth man in the 1923 FA Cup Final and went on to appear in 191 games for the Trotters. On his retirement he was appointed coach to the club's reserve side, later becoming first team coach. In August 1944 he was appointed the club's manager and in his first season in charge, led them to success in the League North Cup. The Wanderers continued to make steady progress under Rowley but in October 1950 he was forced to resign owing to ill-health. He was awarded life membership of the club for services rendered before later returning to management with Middlesbrough in June 1952.

In his first full season in charge, 'Boro finished 13th in the First Division but in 1953–54 with the club struggling against relegation, Rowley was admitted into hospital to undergo treatment for a stomach ulcer. He proffered his resignation to the board whilst in hospital but when the club decided to part company with him, he had made a full recovery and was out of hospital.

Rowley later managed Shrewsbury Town before ending his involvement with the game in 1957.

S

SCHWARZER, MARK

Australian international goalkeeper Mark Schwarzer joined Bradford City from Kaiserslautern in November 1996 for a fee of £350,000. A firm favourite with the Valley Parade faithful, it came as a great surprise when he was allowed to join Middlesbrough for £1.5 million just three months later.

He made his 'Boro debut in the club's 2–0 win against Stockport County at Edgeley Park in the League Cup semi-final first-leg.

The following season he helped the club win promotion to the Premier League, keeping 14 clean sheets in 35 league appearances, despite breaking a leg. After having the last of a steel plate he had inserted in his broken leg removed, Schwarzer gave a number of outstanding performances, saving two penalties and keeping over a dozen clean sheets.

Schwarzer, who had played in 132 first team games up until the end of the 1998–99 season, has recently signed a contract which will keep him at the Riverside Stadium until 2004.

SCOREBOARD

Middlesbrough claim to have had the first half-time scoreboard erected on a Football League ground at the start of the 1902–03 season. The first score it recorded was Middlesbrough leading 1–0 at Blackburn Rovers on 1 September 1902.

SECOND DIVISION

Middlesbrough have had eight spells in the Second Division, the first beginning in 1899–1900 following their admission to the Football League. It lasted for three seasons for in 1901–02, 'Boro won promotion as runners-up to West Bromwich Albion. There followed 18 seasons of top flight football before 'Boro were relegated in 1923–24. Three seasons into their second spell of Second Division football, the club won the Second Division Championship. After just one season in the First Division, 'Boro were relegated but their third spell in Division Two also lasted just one season as they won the Championship for a second time in three seasons. 'Boro's fourth spell of Second Division football began in 1954–55 but this time ended with relegation to Division Three in 1965–66. The club won the Third Division title at the first attempt to begin the 1967–68 season in Division Two. Seven seasons of Second Division culminated with the club winning the Championship in 1973–74, finishing 15 points clear of runners-up Luton Town. 'Boro were relegated in 1981–82 but their sixth spell ended in disaster as they lost their Second Division status four seasons later, being relegated to Division Three. After winning promotion at the first attempt, the club went straight into the First Division, winning a successive promotion in what was their only season in a seventh spell in Division Two. The club's eighth and final spell of Second Division football began in 1989–90 and lasted for three seasons before they won promotion as runners-up to Ipswich Town in 1991–92.

SEMI-FINALS

Up to the end of the 1998–99 season, Middlesbrough had been involved in one FA Cup semi-final and four Football League Cup semi-finals.

SHEPHERDSON, HAROLD

After playing both cricket and football for Yorkshire Boys, Harold Shepherdson signed amateur forms for Middlesbrough before later turning professional. He made his first team debut for 'Boro in a 3–1 defeat at West Bromwich Albion on the final day of the 1936–37 season. Shepherdson found it difficult to hold down a first team place and over four seasons at Ayresome Park, only played in 17 games. In May 1947 he was allowed to leave and join Southend United but before he made his league debut for the Roots Hall club, he suffered a knee injury and was forced to retire.

In 1949, Shepherdson was appointed as Middlesbrough's assistant-trainer, being promoted after the club's trainer Tom Mayson had retired. In 1957 he became England's trainer under Walter Winterbottom and still held the position when the World Cup was won in 1966.

During his time at Ayresome Park, Shepherdson served four periods as the club's caretaker-manager. One of the club's greatest servants, he was awarded a testimonial by the FA in 1973 before retiring ten years later, by which time he was the club's chief executive.

SIMOD CUP

The Simod Cup replaced the Full Members' Cup for the 1987–88 season. 'Boro's first round match that season saw them crash out of the competition when they lost 1–0 at Ipswich Town. In 1988–89 a Dean Glover penalty was enough to beat Oldham Athletic in the opening round and set up a second round meeting with Portsmouth at Fratton Park. 'Boro won 2–1 after extra-Time and then beat Coventry City 1–0 in the third round. Sadly they went down 3–2 at home to Crystal Palace in the fourth round in front of an Ayresome Park crowd of 16,314.

SLAVEN, BERNIE

Much-travelled striker Bernie Slaven played for Morton, Airdrie and Queen of the South before joining Albion Rovers. In 1984–85 Slaven netted 31 times for Albion and was Scotland's top scorer, winning the Golden Shot Trophy. He then refused to re-sign for Albion following a dispute with the club and took it upon himself to write to every First and Second Division side in England asking for a trial.

'Boro's Willie Maddren responded and eventually signed Slaven for £25,000. He made his league debut in a 1–0 defeat at Leeds United in October 1985 but then scored on his first game at Ayresome Park as 'Boro drew 1–1 with Bradford City. Though the club were relegated at the end of that campaign, Slaven was instrumental in 'Boro winning promotion from the Third Division at the first attempt, top-scoring with 17 goals.

He also netted his first hat-trick in a 3–0 FA Cup win over Blackpool. In 1987–88 when the club won promotion to the First Division via the play-offs, Slaven again top-scored with 21 goals including hat-tricks in the wins over Huddersfield Town (Away 4–1) and Shrewsbury Town (Home 4–0). In the top flight, Slaven continued to find the net on a regular basis and was the club's top scorer for a third successive season with 15

goals including a hat-trick in a 4–3 win at Coventry City.

Slaven was the club's top scorer for six successive seasons, netting 21 goals in 1989–90 when he was ever-present. Though 'Boro were relegated, Slaven was rewarded with selection for the Republic of Ireland, qualifying through his Irish grandfather. He was a member of Jack Charlton's World Cup squad in Italy that year, but not used.

In 1990–91, Slaven scored 16 goals including his fifth hat-trick for the club in a 4–2 win at Brighton and Hove Albion. In 'Boro's promotion-winning season of 1991–92, Slaven was used more as a substitute, making only 28 starts. His total of 16 goals included another treble against Brighton in a 4–0 home win. The following season his first team appearances became even more infrequent and before the campaign had ended, Slaven, who had scored 146 goals in 381 games, moved to Port Vale.

He helped the Valiants win the Autoglass Trophy before returning to the north-east with Darlington where a back injury forced his retirement.

SMALLEST PLAYER

Although such statistics are always unreliable for those playing around the turn of the century, the distinction of being Middlesbrough's smallest player goes to Arthur Kaye. The former Blackpool winger who began his career with his home-town team, Barnsley stood 5ft 3ins.

SOUNESS, GRAEME

A Scottish Schoolboy and Youth international, he signed apprentice forms for Spurs in 1969 and turned professional the following year. However, with established midfielders of the quality of Alan Mullery, Martin Peters and Steve Perryman, the young Souness grew frustrated. Though he was a substitute in two league games, his only first team appearance for the White Hart Lane club was in a UEFA Cup match against Keflavik of Iceland. After playing for Montreal Olympic in the NASL he made his frustration clear and even walked out on the club.

Reluctantly, Spurs allowed him to move to Middlesbrough for £32,000 and from there he went on to develop into one of the game's most influential performers of modern times.

He made his 'Boro debut in a 2–1 defeat at Fulham in 1973 but by the end of that season he had established himself as a first team regular in the Ayresome Park club's side. In 1973–74 his first full season with the club, he helped them win promotion to the First Division and won his first Scotland Under-23 cap. In October 1974 he won his first full

honours and had added another two full caps to his total by the time of his major transfer to Liverpool.

Souness, who had scored 23 goals in 204 League and Cup games, cost Liverpool £352,000. At Anfield he blossomed into a world-class player. He had the ability to totally dominate games, taking control and dictating the play with his strength and pin-point passing. With Liverpool he won almost every honour the game can offer - League Championship medals in 1979, 1980, 1982, 1983 and 1984, League Cup Winners' medals in 1981, 1982, 1983 and 1984, European Cup winners' medals in 1978, 1981 and 1984 and 37 more Scottish caps.

Having reached the pinnacle at English football, he turned his attention to Europe and moved to Sampdoria of Italy, where he spent two successful years, picking up another 14 Scottish caps. In April 1986 he returned to Britain as player-manager of Rangers. In his first season, the Ibrox club won the Scottish League and Scottish League Cup. Part-owner of Rangers, Souness was still striving for the only major trophy to elude Rangers, the European Cup, when he left in April 1991 to become manager of Liverpool.

After the shock of undergoing major heart surgery, he led them to the one trophy he failed to capture as a player, the FA Cup. Since then, Souness has managed Turkish giants Galatasaray and Southampton but after a spell in charge at Benfica is now manager at Blackburn Rovers.

SPONSORS

The club's present sponsors are Cellnet. Previous sponsors have included Datsun, Cleveland, McLean Homes, Camerons Ales, Dickens, Heritage Hampers, ICI and Evening Gazette. British Steel withdrew their sponsorship of Middlesbrough when they discovered that only 2,000 tonnes of British steel were used in the construction of the Riverside Stadium. The other 18,000 tonnes were imported from Germany.

SPRAGGON, FRANK

After progressing through the club's junior and reserve ranks, defender Frank Spraggon made his Middlesbrough debut in a League Cup tie against Bradford City in October 1963. However, over the next four seasons, Spraggon made only 20 first team appearances and had to wait until 1967–68 before playing on a regular basis. From then on he missed very few games, with the exception of 1971–72 when a cartilage operation and blurred vision kept him out of the side. Following the emergence of Willie

Maddren at wing-half, Spraggon moved to left-back and continued to give the club good service until 1976.

Spraggon, who had played in 322 League and Cup games for 'Boro went to play for Minnesota Kicks in the NASL. On his return to England, he signed for Hartlepool United but after only one League appearance for them, he damaged his knee and was forced to retire.

He now works at Middlesbrough's School of Excellence.

SPUHLER, JOHNNY

Sunderland-born winger Johnny Spuhler won England Schoolboy honours before being taken on to the office staff of his home-town club. The Wearsiders eventually offered him professional terms but during the Second World War, he 'guested' for Middlesbrough. In October 1945, 'Boro manager David Jack paid £1,750 to bring Spuhler to Ayresome Park on a permanent basis.

He made his League debut for the club in the 1–0 win at Aston Villa on the opening day of the 1946–47 season, ending the campaign with 10 goals in 32 games. His total included a spell of three games in which he scored twice in each match - Blackpool (Away 5–0), Brentford (Home 2–0), and Leeds United (Away 3–3). He also netted four goals that season in the club's run to the sixth round of the FA Cup. Over the next eight seasons, Spuhler continued to score on a regular basis with a best league return of 13 in 35 games in 1950–51 when 'Boro finished sixth in Division One. He had scored 81 goals in 241 League and Cup games when following 'Boro's relegation to the Second Division, he was allowed to join Darlington for £1,000.

His stay at the Feethams was brief, Spuhler becoming player-manager of Spennymoor United. He later entered League management with Shrewsbury Town before ending his involvement with the game as full-time coach to Stockton FC.

STILES, NOBBY

Nobby Stiles captained Manchester Boys and played for England Schoolboys before making his debut for Manchester United as an 18 year-old at Bolton in October 1960. He went on to play in 392 games in 14 years at Old Trafford, winning two League Championship medals and a European Cup winners' medal.

Stiles, who won 28 full caps for his country, was a star of England's 1966 World Cup win and will always be remembered for his chirpy,

toothless smile following the 4–2 defeat of West Germany.

In 1971, Stiles moved to Middlesbrough for £20,000 and made his debut in a 2–1 defeat at Portsmouth on the opening day of the 1971–72 season. Over the next two seasons, Stiles, who had been appointed captain, appeared in 69 games for 'Boro but in the summer of 1973 after helping the club finish fourth in Division Two, he discovered he wasn't part of new manager Jack Charlton's plans and joined his former United colleague and Jack's brother, Bobby at Preston North End.

Nobby Stiles

Stiles was North End manager when the Deepdale club won promotion to Division Two in 1976–77 but after being unable to bring further glory to the Lilywhites, he had a spell coaching in the USA before joining brother-in-law Johnny Giles at West Bromwich Albion. He left the Hawthorns at the end of the 1988–89 season and returned to Old Trafford where he coached the youth team before becoming the co-director of United's School of Excellence from 1989 to 1995.

STUART, BOBBY

An England Schoolboy international, Bobby Stuart began his Football League career with Middlesbrough. Despite dislocating his shoulder in his first game in 'Boro's colours whilst playing for the reserves, he recovered to make his League debut at Arsenal in April 1932.

Despite being on the wrong end of a 5–0 scoreline that day, Stuart kept his place in the side and was a first team regular up until the outbreak of the Second World War.

During the hostilities, Stuart captained the club in the majority of the 133 matches in which he played. He was still a member of the club's first team when League football resumed in 1946–47. He took his total of appearances in League and Cup games to 268 before he was transferred to Plymouth Argyle along with George Dews.

He appeared in 20 league games for the Pilgrims before becoming coach to non-League Whitby, a position he held for two years before ending his involvement with the game.

SUBSTITUTES

Middlesbrough's first substitute was Bryan Orritt, who came on for Neville Chapman in the club's seventh game of the 1965–66 season in a 1–1 draw against Preston North End at Deepdale. The club's first goalscoring Number 12 was John O'Rourke who scored in 'Boro's 2–0 win at Hull City on 23 September 1967.

The greatest number of substitutes used in a single season by 'Boro under the single-substitute rule was 30 in 1981–82. From 1986–87, two substitutes were allowed and in 1991–92, the club used 60. In recent seasons, three substitutes have been allowed and in 1997–98, the Riverside club used 76.

The greatest number of substitute appearances for Middlesbrough in a season is 18, a feat achieved by Alan Kernaghan in 1988–89.

SUNDERLAND

Middlesbrough played their first game against Sunderland during the 1887–88 season. The occasion was the third qualifying round of the FA Cup and the match was played at Linthorpe Road. Sunderland were leading 2–0 but early in the second-half, Middlesbrough pulled a goal back before equalising in the closing minutes to earn a 2–2 draw.

When the teams replayed at Newcastle Road, it was Middlesbrough who went into a 2–0 lead but the Wearsiders came back strongly to win 4–2. Middlesbrough protested about the professionalism of three Scots, members of the Sunderland side. At an inquiry held in Darlington, the commission suspended the players concerned, threw Sunderland out of the competition and reinstated Middlesbrough. After beating Old Foresters, 'Boro lost to Crewe Alexandra in the quarter-finals.

The clubs first met in the Football League in 1902–03. The Wearsiders won 1–0 at Middlesbrough and then completed the 'double' over 'Boro, winning 2–1 in the return which was played at St James Park after Sunderland's Roker Park had been closed due to crowd trouble.

In 1913–14, 'Boro lost both League meetings but in going down 4–3 at home, George Elliott became the first Middlesbrough player to score a hat-trick in the fixture. In 1920–21, 'Boro completed the 'double' over the Wearsiders for the first time, winning 2–0 at Ayresome Park and 2–1 at Roker Park. Results over the next few seasons were mixed but on 28 March 1936, champions-elect Sunderland visited Ayresome Park and were severely beaten 6–0.

The Wearsiders had both Carter and Davis sent-off, whilst 'Boro's goals were scored by Birkett(2), Camsell, Cunliffe, Higham and Yorston (penalty). The following season the clubs drew 5–5 at Ayresome Park with George Camsell netting a hat-trick for 'Boro.

In 1938–39 the two clubs met in the FA Cup for the first time in over 50 years, Sunderland winning 2–0 in front of an Ayresome Park ground attendance record of 51,080.

The 100th Tees-Wear derby game took place at Roker Park on 3 April 1982 and though 'Boro were to end the season at the bottom of the First Division, they won 2–0 with goals from Ashcroft and Baxter. The two clubs last played each other on 21 February 1998 when 'Boro won 3–1 with two goals from Branca and another from Armstrong.

They also won 2–1 at the Stadium of Light and defeated the Wearsiders 2–0 in the third round of that season's League Cup competition.

160

Middlesbrough's record against Sunderland in the various competitions is as follows:

	P	W	D	L	F	A
Football League	114	33	30	51	144	177
FA Cup	4	1	1	2	7	9
Football League Cup	5	3	1	1	7	3
Anglo-Scottish Cup	1	1	0	0	3	2
TOTAL	124	38	32	54	161	191

SUSTAINED SCORING

During the 1926–27 season when Middlesbrough won the Second Division Championship, George Camsell scored 59 goals in 37 league games after being left out of the opening four matches of the season, of which 'Boro drew one and lost three. He scored 29 goals in 12 consecutive league games including all five in a 5–3 win at Manchester City and four in the wins over Portsmouth (Home 7–3), Fulham (Home 6–1), and Swansea Town (Home 7–1).

T

TALLEST PLAYER

It is impossible to say for definite who has been the tallest player ever on Middlesbrough's books as such records are notoriously unreliable. But almost certain to lay claim to the distinction is the club's Australian international goalkeeper Mark Schwarzer who is 6ft 5ins.

TAYLOR, PETER

Peter Taylor found fame as Brian Clough's assistant at Derby County and Nottingham Forest, winning honours galore at both clubs.

Taylor began his career as a goalkeeper and after a short spell on the books of Forest, he joined Coventry City. After making 90 appearances for the Highfield Road club, he was signed by Middlesbrough in the summer of 1955. He made his debut in a 2–2 draw at Hull City in October 1955 and after eventually replacing Rolando Ugolini as the club's first-choice 'keeper he went on to appear in 146 games over the next four seasons. After losing his place to Bob Appleby, he left Ayresome Park to join Port Vale. He had made just one league appearance for the Valiants when he decided to retire.

He was managing Southern League Burton Albion whilst teaching Physical Education on a part-time basis at a local school when Clough asked him to join him at Hartlepool. After moving to Derby in 1967, they took the Rams to the Second Division title in 1968–69, followed by the club's first League Championship in 1971–72.

Both men resigned from their posts at the Baseball Ground amidst great controversy and though they later continued their partnership at Brighton, Clough soon left to take charge at Leeds United. Taylor joined up with Clough again at the City Ground, taking Forest to the League Championship in 1977–78, the League Cup in 1977–78 and 1978–79 and the European Cup in 1978–79 and 1979–80. In 1981 came an acrimonious split which sadly was never healed before Taylor's death in 1990. He later came out of retirement to manage Derby County. He helped the Rams out of trouble with a remarkable run-in to the season before they were relegated to the Third Division a year later.

TEXACO CUP
The predecessor to the Anglo-Scottish Cup, the Texaco Cup was launched in 1970–71 and was for English, Irish and Scottish club sides not involved in European competitions that season. Middlesbrough only participated in 1974–75 but after the following qualifying round results - Carlisle United (Home 0–1), Sunderland (Away 1–0), and Newcastle United (Away 0–4) - failed to reach the knockout stages.

THIRD DIVISION
Middlesbrough have had two spells in the Third Division, each lasting just one season and each ending with promotion to Division Two as the club finished in the runners-up position.

'Boro's first season in the Third Division was 1966–67 when, after winning 3–2 at Colchester United on the opening day of the season, they managed only one more win in their next nine matches. It seemed as if the club would be heading straight down to the Fourth Division but new signings John O'Rourke and John Hickton began to find the net and after an 11–match unbeaten run of which eight matches ended in victory, 'Boro were on the fringe of the promotion pack. After winning four and drawing one of five games in 21 days, 'Boro entertained Oxford United on the final day of the season, needing to win to overtake both Watford and Reading who had completed their games and take the second promotion place. Win they did, 4–1 with John O'Rourke who top-scored with 27 goals, netting a hat-trick.

'Boro's second season in the Third Division was 1986–87 but because the club had been issued with a winding-up order, they played their first game against Port Vale as an evening kick-off at Hartlepool United's ground to comply with the Football League's ruling. That game ended

all-square at 2–2 but 'Boro then went ten matches before being defeated 3–1 at home by Blackpool. The club remained in the promotion race throughout the season and ended the campaign with a 13–match unbeaten run to guarantee promotion to the Second Division as runners-up to Bournemouth.

TODD, COLIN

Colin Todd was an elegant and poised player who was always comfortable on the ball. He developed a great partnership with Roy McFarland at Derby which was later transferred into the England team. Todd won two League Championship medals with the Rams and in 1974–75 was voted the PFA Footballer of the Year. He later helped Birmingham City win promotion to the First Division and Oxford United to the Third Division Championship. After managing Whitley Bay he became assistant-manager to Bruce Rioch at Middlesbrough, eventually succeeding him as manager in March 1990.

Employed too late to save the club from relegation he took 'Boro to the Second Division play-offs in 1991 after finishing seventh, but lost to Notts County in the semi-final.

In May 1991 he resigned and a year later became Rioch's assistant again, this time at Bolton Wanderers. He played an important part in the club's promotion to the Premier League and in Wanderers' cup exploits, culminating in them reaching the League Cup Final in 1995. When Rioch left, Todd stayed at the club as assistant to newly appointed Roy McFarland but in January 1996 when he was sacked, Todd became manager. Though he couldn't prevent their relegation, he led Wanderers to the First Division Championship in 1996–97 and to the play-offs in 1998–99 following their relegation the previous season. In September 1999 he resigned his post at the Reebok Stadium following the sale, against his wishes, of Danish international Per Frandsen to Blackburn Rovers. Todd has recently been appointed manager of Swindon Town.

TOURS

Middlesbrough's first-ever tour was in May 1907 when they embarked on a two-match tour of Denmark. After beating the Danish University 5–3, they drew 2–2 with a Danish XI. 'Boro visited Denmark again at the end of the following season and gained revenge by beating a Denmark XI 5–2. The club's third tour of Denmark in May 1927 saw them lose 4–2 in the first of two matches against a Danish XI but then

win 8–2 against the same opposition four days later with George Camsell scoring five of the goals.

Since then, 'Boro have toured a number of other countries including Norway, Iceland, Holland, Switzerland, Germany, Australia, New Zealand and North America.

In the summer of 1980, 'Boro embarked on an ambitious World tour, playing in Japan, Argentina, China, Spain, Morocco and Greece - winning four and drawing three of their eight matches, with their only defeat being 4–0 against Panathinaikos.

One of the club's biggest wins on tour was the 8–0 defeat of Northern New South Wales on 18 May 1975 when manager Jack Charlton played and scored two goals!

TOWNSEND, ANDY

After starting his career with Welling United in the Southern League, he joined Weymouth, thus stepping up one grade to what was then the Gola League. After only half a season with the Dorset club, his performances attracted the attention of Southampton who signed him in January 1985 for £35,000.

He did not make an immediate impact in the top flight and had to wait until the end of the season before making his debut at left-back in a 2–0 win over Aston Villa. In 1985–86 he alternated between left-back and midfield but missed the first half of the following season after breaking a leg in a pre-season friendly against his old club, Weymouth. In 1987–88 he established himself as a commanding midfield player but in the summer of 1988 he was rather surprisingly sold to Norwich City. He helped the Canaries to their highest-ever league position of fourth in Division One and to the semi-finals of the FA Cup.

He also won international recognition with the Republic of Ireland, making his debut against France in February 1989. After one more season at Carrow Road he was transferred to Chelsea for £1.2 million but after three years in which he confirmed his reputation as one of the leading midfield operators in the top flight, he joined Aston Villa for £2 million.

A tremendous competitor, he made 176 appearances for Villa before signing for Middlesbrough for a fee of £500,000 in the summer of 1997. He made his debut as a substitute for the Brazilian Emerson in a 2–0 win at Tranmere Rovers in the third game of the 1997–98 season, going on to play in 37 games as 'Boro won promotion to the Premier League.

Andy Townsend

Back in the top flight, Townsend, who won 70 caps for the Republic of Ireland, was appointed club captain and took his total of appearances for Middlesbrough to 83 in a season in which he was almost ever-present.

TRANSFERS

Middlesbrough's purchase of Alf Common from Sunderland scandalised the country. They were struggling to avoid relegation from the First Division and had not won an away game for more than two years but so many people thought that did not justify them spending the unheard sum of £1,000 on the England inside-forward. Common scored on his debut at Sheffield United to bring Middlesbrough a long awaited away win. The FA then passed a rule limiting transfer fees to £350 and fining Middlesbrough for making unauthorised payments to players. 'Boro fans were not bothered as Common's arrival helped the club to escape relegation.

The record transfer fee received by the club was £12 million that Atletico Madrid paid for Juninho in July 1997. The record transfer fee paid out by Middlesbrough was £7 million to Juventus for Fabrizio Ravanelli in August 1996.

U

UGOLINI, ROLANDO

Rolando Ugolini was born in Lucca, Italy but moved with his family to Scotland when he was a youngster. It was here that he first came to the attention of the football scouts and after being on the books of Hearts, was signed by Celtic. The Second World War interrupted his playing career but when he did get back to playing, it was mainly as an understudy to Scottish international goalkeeper Willie Millar.

In May 1948 after turning down a move to Chelsea he joined Middlesbrough and made his debut in a 1–0 defeat against the Stamford Bridge club on the opening day of the 1948–49 season. Nicknamed 'Rolando the Cat' he was 'Boro's first choice 'keeper for eight seasons, being ever-present in 1950–51 and 1953–54. He had appeared in 335 League and Cup games when he lost his place in the side to Peter Taylor and after a season playing reserve team football, joined Wrexham.

He helped the Welsh club gain Third Division status when the North and South regions were amalgamated to make Divisions Three and Four in 1958. He played in 93 games for Wrexham before at the age of 36 headed back to Scotland to play for Dundee United where he ended his career.

UNDEFEATED

Middlesbrough's longest run of undefeated Football League matches both home and away is 24 between 8 September 1973 and 9 January 1974. 'Boro's best and longest undefeated home sequence in the Football

League is of 27 matches between 8 February 1936 and 10 April 1937, coming to an end when they lost 3–1 to Derby County.

URWIN, TOMMY

A former England Schoolboy international, Tommy Urwin played non-League football for Lambton Star and Shildon before joining Middlesbrough as an amateur in February 1914. After turning professional he made his first team debut for 'Boro in a 3–2 home defeat by Sunderland on New Year's Day 1915. Urwin established himself as a first team regular in the Middlesbrough side when League football resumed in 1919–20 and was a virtual ever-present for the next five seasons. However, when 'Boro were relegated in 1923–24, Urwin, who had scored 14 goals in 200 games left to join Newcastle United.

He helped the Magpies win the League Championship in 1926–27 and represented the Football League during his stay at St James Park. He also made 200 appearances for Newcastle, scoring 24 goals before moving to the third big north-east club, Sunderland. He made 85 appearances for the Wearsiders before hanging up his boots. He remained at Roker Park as the club's youth team coach, later acting as a scout for the Wearsiders.

UTILITY PLAYERS

A utility player is one of those particularly gifted footballers who can play in several or even many different positions. One of the club's earliest utility players was Bob Baxter who captained the side in the years leading up to the outbreak of the Second World War. Though the majority of his 266 games were played at centre-half, the Scottish international appeared in eight different numbered outfield shirts. Ronnie Dicks played for Middlesbrough during the Second World War but had to wait until 1947–48 before making his league debut. He wore nine different numbered outfield shirts and was known as 'The Handyman' of Ayresome Park. Bryan Orritt played in all 11 positions for the club during his five seasons at Ayresome Park and was 'Boro's first playing substitute.

After the mid 1960s, players were encouraged to become more adaptable and to see their roles as less stereotyped. At the same time, much less attention was paid to the implications of wearing a certain numbered shirt. Accordingly, some of the more versatile players came to wear all the different numbered shirts at some stage or another although this did not necessarily indicate a vast variety of position. Irving Nattrass and Tony McAndrew both proved their versatility, occupying nine different positions.

V

VICKERS, STEVE

Bishop Auckland-born defender Steve Vickers joined Tranmere Rovers from Spennymoor in 1985 after turning down Middlesbrough!

Vickers made his league debut for Tranmere in a 3–1 home defeat by Northampton Town in April 1986, establishing himself as the club's first choice centre-half the following season. Vickers who was ever-present in season's 1987–88 and 1988–89 appeared in 148 consecutive games for Rovers during this period and missed very few games in eight seasons at Prenton Park.

He won a Leyland Daf Cup winners' medal in 1989 and made 387 League and Cup appearances as the Wirral club rose from the old Fourth Division to become perennial play-off candidates in Division One.

Vickers eventually left Prenton Park in December 1993, joining Middlesbrough for £700,000. Making his 'Boro debut as a substitute in a goalless draw at Bristol City, he was an important member of the side that won the First Division Championship in 1994–95. During that season his performances alongside Nigel Pearson and Derek Whyte at the heart of the 'Boro defence won him the supporters' Player of the Year award. He continued to build on his immense popularity on Teeside with a series of outstanding performances in 1996–97, helping the club reach both FA and League Cup Finals where he appeared in both matches as a substitute.

The versatile and powerful defender was the cornerstone of 'Boro's

well established defence, only missing games through injury, he was again prominent in the club's return to the top flight at the first attempt. In the Premiership he took his total of first team appearances for 'Boro to 237, displaying complete competence in all aspects of his role.

VICTORIES IN A SEASON - HIGHEST
In the 1986–87 season, Middlesbrough won 28 of their 46 league fixtures and finished runners-up in the Third Division, the highest number of wins in a season in the club's history.

VICTORIES IN A SEASON - LOWEST
Middlesbrough's poorest performance was in 1923–24 when they won seven matches out of their 42 league games and finished bottom of the First Division.

WALKER, ANDY

Former Airdrie manager Andy Walker was appointed manager of Middlesbrough in the summer of 1910 but did not get off to the best of starts at Ayresome Park, being suspended for four weeks for an illegal approach to one of his former players. There was even more trouble a few months later when 'Boro chairman Thomas Gibson-Poole, a local Tory parliamentary candidate wanted the club to beat local rivals Sunderland in an attempt to further his chances of being elected at the forthcoming elections. The Middlesbrough boss was used to offer Sunderland's captain Charlie Thomson £30 to throw the match. Thomson reported the incident to his own chairman and an FA Commission was set up to investigate the matter.

In January 1911 both Walker and Gibson-Poole were permanently suspended from the game. Many people believed Walker had been used by his chairman and though a petition was presented to the FA for his reinstatement, it wasn't successful.

However, the ban was eventually lifted and Walker returned to management with Barrow.

WALKER, GEOFF

Bradford-born winger Geoff Walker played his early football during the Second World War with his home-town club before Middlesbrough manager David Jack signed him from Park Avenue in the summer of 1946.

He made his debut for 'Boro in a 1–0 win at Aston Villa on the opening day of the 1946–47 season and went on to be a first team regular for the next eight seasons. Though his dangerous crosses created many a goalscoring opportunity for his colleagues, he also possessed a powerful shot and in 259 League and Cup appearances, scored 53 goals with a best of 11 in 1947–48.

Following 'Boro's relegation to the Second Division, Walker left to join Doncaster Rovers who were also in Division Two. He stayed with the Belle Vue club for two seasons, scoring 15 goals in 84 games before moving back to his home-town, this time to sign for Bradford City. His stay at Valley Parade was brief and he moved into non-League football with Clacton Town before hanging up his boots.

WALKER, JOHN

Beith-born defender John Walker played his early football with Burnbank Athletic before joining Raith Rovers. During his time with the Stark's Park club, he suffered a bad leg injury and as matters were not improving following treatment by the club's trainer, he sought advice from his counterpart at Celtic. Though he was advised to rest, Raith were not sympathetic and suspended him for visiting Parkhead.

Walker said he would never play for Raith again and after regaining full fitness, joined Rangers. After a couple of seasons at Ibrox, he moved south of the border to play for Swindon Town in the Southern League. Whilst with the Wiltshire club he helped them win the Southern League Championship and won nine full caps for Scotland.

He joined Middlesbrough in the summer of 1913 and played his first game for the club in a 1–1 draw at Manchester City on the opening day of the 1913–14 season. He was a regular in the 'Boro side up to the outbreak of the First World War and was still the club's first-choice when League football resumed in 1919–20. Walker went on to appear in 109 games before leaving to end his career with Reading.

WAR

Middlesbrough lost a number of players fighting for the country. During the First World War, former Celtic star Don McLeod, who had played in 148 games at full-back for 'Boro, Archie Wilson who had scored four goals in 23 games during 1914–15 and the promising young centre-half, Andrew Jackson who had already played in 137 games, all lost their lives.

WARTIME FOOTBALL

Despite the outbreak of the First World War in 1914, the major football leagues embarked upon their planned programme of matches for the ensuing season and these were completed on schedule at the end of April the following year when Middlesbrough finished 12th in Division One. Sadly, the outbreak of war brought about the deaths of three Middlesbrough players, killed in the hostilities - Andrew Jackson, Archie Wilson and Don McLeod. Ayresome Park became a military training centre and the club closed down until the 1918–19 season when it joined the Northern Victory League. Introduced as a preliminary to the start of the new Football League season, 'Boro were champions with the following record:

P	W	D	L	F	A	Pts
14	9	2	3	28	12	20

In complete contrast to the events of 1914, once war was declared on 3 September 1939, the Football League programme of 1939–40 was suspended and for a while there was no football of any description. The game continued on a regional basis and Middlesbrough entered the North Eastern Regional League. The following seven seasons brought some unusual results - in 1939–40 'Boro beat Darlington 8–1 at Ayresome Park but lost 8–0 at the Feethams! Also a number of 'guest' players turned out for 'Boro during the hostilities, they included Matt Busby (Liverpool), Johnny Carey (Manchester United), Bill Nicholson (Tottenham Hotspur), and Alec Herd (Manchester City).

WATSON, JIMMY

Nicknamed 'Daddy Long Legs' Jimmy Watson began his football career with Burnbank, a Lanarkshire junior side. After turning down an offer to play for Hearts, he signed for Clyde where his displays at full-back quickly brought him to the attention of Sunderland who secured his services in January 1900.

His first game for the Wearsiders was in a goalless home draw against Glossop North End, a month after joining the club. Watson spent eight seasons at Roker Park, appearing in 225 League and Cup games and winning a League Championship medal in 1901–02.

The tough-tackling defender also won four full caps for Scotland with three of his international appearances coming against the Auld Enemy.

In April 1907, Watson moved to Middlesbrough and made his debut in a 2–0 home win over Manchester United. He was ever-present in 1907–08 when the club finished sixth in Division One, his form earning him two more caps for Scotland. He had appeared in 107 games for 'Boro when at the end of the 1909–10 season, he decided to retire from League football. He then had a spell as 'Boro's assistant-trainer before playing non-League football for Shildon.

He later emigrated to Canada and in the years immediately following the First World War he was coaching in that country.

WAYMAN, CHARLIE

Charlie Wayman was born in Bishop Auckland and started his working life in the coal mines. After playing for Chilton Colliery and Spennymoor United, he joined Newcastle United for whom he proved to be a prolific scorer in the War Leagues.

When League football resumed in 1946, Wayman was a regular in the Magpies' forward line and in that season topped the Second Division scoring charts with 30 goals as well as netting a hat-trick to knock Southampton out of the FA Cup. Surprisingly he was allowed to leave St James Park and in October 1947, Southampton manager Bill Dodgin paid £10,000 to take Wayman to The Dell. Settling in immediately, he scored 17 goals in 27 games as the Saints ended the season in third place in Division Two. The following season he scored five goals in a 6–0 win over Leicester City, a club record that still stands today. In 1949–50, Wayman scored 24 goals in 36 league games including a hat-trick in a 5–0 home win over Hull City but the Saints ended the season on 52 points as did both Sheffield clubs. Tottenham were the champions and Sheffield Wednesday were promoted with them on goal average.

Wayman's wife had never really settled in the south and after scoring 81 goals in 107 games he moved to Preston North End. In his first season with the Deepdale club he scored four goals in the first-half against Queen's Park Rangers at Loftus Road on Christmas Day, ending the campaign with 27 goals. His flair for goals earned him a memorable hat-trick against Arsenal at Highbury. During North End's FA Cup run of 1954, the courageous Wayman scored in every round including the final against West Bromwich Albion.

In September 1954, Middlesbrough manager Bob Dennison paid £8,000 to take Wayman to Ayresome Park and he made his debut in a 2–1 home win over Lincoln City. He ended the season as the club's top

scorer with 17 goals including four in the 6–0 home defeat of West Ham United. The following season he took his tally of goals for 'Boro to 33 in 58 games, netting a hat-trick in a 4–0 win at Barnsley.

He later ended his career at Darlington where he took his total of league goals to 254 in 382 appearances for his five clubs.

Charlie Wayman

WEATHER CONDITIONS

On Saturday 1 September 1906, Middlesbrough played Everton in the First Division at Ayresome Park. Wilcox and Barker scored for 'Boro in a 2–2 draw on what is thought to be the hottest day on which the league programme has ever been completed - the temperature was over 90F (32C).

WEBSTER, MAURICE

Blackpool-born centre-half Maurice Webster served in France with the 4th Duke of Wellington's Regiment in the First World War. When the hostilities were over he played for Lytham in the West Lancashire League before joining Fleetwood in the Lancashire Combination. In 1921 Webster signed professional forms for Stalybridge Celtic. He had been with the Cheshire side for less than a year when Middlesbrough paid £1,500 for his services in March 1922.

He made his league debut for 'Boro in a 2–1 defeat at Huddersfield Town towards the end of the 1921–22 season, establishing himself as a first team regular midway through the following campaign. With the exception of 1926–27 and 1927–28 when he played in just a handful of games in each campaign, Webster was Middlesbrough's first choice pivot until 1932–33.

His form led to him playing in an England trial game where he completely dominated his battle with 'Boro team-mate George Camsell. Webster won three full caps for England, breaking his nose on his final appearance against Germany in Berlin.

He had appeared in 281 League and Cup games for Middlesbrough when he left to play for Carlisle United. Sadly he broke his leg during his first season with the Brunton Park club, an injury which ended his playing career. He stayed with the Cumbrian side until 1948, working as the club's trainer before becoming coach and groundsman with Stockton FC.

WHIGHAM, WILLIE

Goalkeeper Willie Whigham began his career with Falkirk whom he helped win promotion from the Scottish First Division in 1960–61. Whigham spent five seasons at Brockville Park where his outstanding displays prompted 'Boro manager Stan Anderson to pay £10,000 for his services in October 1966.

He went straight into the Middlesbrough side, making his debut in a 2–0 defeat at Watford. He kept his place in the side, keeping 13 clean sheets in 35 appearances as 'Boro won promotion to the Second Division. Over the next four seasons, Whigham missed very few games and in 1970–71 was ever-present as the club finished seventh in Division Two.

Though he could occasionally be somewhat erratic, Whigham made 210 appearances for 'Boro before returning to his native Scotland to play for Dumbarton. He later returned to the Football League to play in four games for Darlington.

WHITAKER, BILLY

Chesterfield-born centre-half Billy Whitaker began his career with his home-town club, making his first team debut during the 1942–43 wartime regional league. He had made just 13 Football League appearances for the Spireites when the competition resumed in 1946–47 before leaving to join Middlesbrough for £9,500 at the end of the season.

He made his debut in the 2–2 draw at home to Manchester United on the opening day of the 1947–48 season and was the club's first-choice pivot for the next six seasons. Whitaker also captained 'Boro during this period and scored his only goal for the club in a 3–2 defeat at Burnley in April 1950.

Damaged knee ligaments forced him to miss the whole of the 1953–54 campaign and then a cartilage operation early the following season forced him into retirement. Whitaker who had appeared in 184 League and Cup games for 'Boro also represented the Football League against the Irish League in Belfast in 1950.

WHYTE, DEREK

Glasgow-born central defender Derek Whyte began his career with Celtic and in seven years with the Parkhead club, the Scottish international won a Scottish Premier Division Championship medal and two Scottish Cup winners' medals.

He had appeared in 276 games for Celtic when Middlesbrough persuaded him to join the Teeside club in August 1992. He made his first team debut in a 2–1 defeat at Coventry City on the opening day of the 1992–93 Premier League season, going on to appear in 35 games. A virtual ever-present over the next two seasons, he helped the club win the First Division Championship in 1994–95 and after some sterling displays the following season as the club returned to the top flight, won selection for Scotland's 1996 European Championship squad.

In 1996–97 he played a major role in the club's two cup runs and though 'Boro lost their Premier League status, it wasn't for the want of trying on Derek Whyte's part - his strong running out of defence and good distribution being the main features of his play.

He had played in 195 games for 'Boro when in December 1997 he was transferred to Aberdeen. Though he was selected for Craig Brown's Scotland World Cup squad in France, he failed to make an appearance as the Scots crashed out of the tournament at the group stage.

WILKINSON, PAUL

Paul Wilkinson worked his way up through the ranks at Grimsby Town before making his first team debut for the Mariners. He went on to score 33 goals in 87 games before Everton paid £250,000 to take him to Goodison Park.

Unable to establish himself as a first team regular with the Merseyside

club, Wilkinson moved to Nottingham Forest but after just one season at the City Ground, he was on the move again. Watford paid £300,000 for Wilkinson's services and he repaid them with 56 goals in 155 games in three seasons at Vicarage Road.

Middlesbrough splashed out £550,000 to bring Wilkinson to Ayresome Park and he made his debut in a 1–0 home win over Millwall on the opening day of the 1991–92 season. An ever-present, Wilkinson went on to score 15 goal in 46 games, helping 'Boro to win promotion to the newly-formed Premier League. He was the club's leading scorer for the next two seasons and in 1994–95 netted his only hat-trick for the club in a 4–1 League Cup win over Scarborough. His appearances for 'Boro were curtailed by a series of injuries and after loan spells with Oldham Athletic, Watford and Luton Town, he was freed in the summer of 1996 after scoring 66 goals in 202 games.

He joined Barnsley where he linked up well with former 'Boro favourite John Hendrie, the two strikers helping the Oakwell club win promotion to the Premier League. Despite an outstanding season he had to make way for newcomers and was allowed to join Millwall for £150,000. After one season with the Lions, he was given a free transfer and moved to Northampton Town where sadly his first season at the Sixfields Stadium was hampered by operations on his ankle.

Paul Wilkinson

WILLIAMS, OWEN

Owen Williams began his career with Sunderland but failing to make the grade with the Roker Park club, he left to join Manchester United. Things didn't go his way at Old Trafford either and so he returned to the north-east to play non-League football for Easington Colliery.

His performances led to Clapton Orient offering him the chance to play League football and he went on to be a regular in their side for four seasons after the end of the First World War.

Williams joined Middlesbrough in February 1924 and made his first team debut in a 1–0 defeat at home to West Bromwich Albion. He played in 13 games at the end of that season but was unable to prevent 'Boro's relegation to the Second Division. He was a regular member of the Middlesbrough side for the next five seasons and in 1926–27 helped them win the Second Division Championship when his pin-point crosses from the left-wing helped George Camsell to reach his record total of 59 goals. Despite 'Boro's relegation the following season, Williams won another Second Division Championship medal in 1928–29. He went on to score 44 goals in 194 games before leaving to play for Southend United.

WILLIAMSON, TIM

The holder of the club appearance record, goalkeeper Tim Williamson first played for the club in a friendly match against Cliftonville after impressing for the Redcar Crusaders. His display in the friendly match was outstanding but Williamson would only sign professional forms for the club if they agreed to allow him to continue qualifying as a draughtsman! Thankfully they agreed and Williamson made his league debut in a 2–0 home win over Bristol City in April 1902. It was midway through the following season before he established himself as the club's first choice 'keeper - a position he held until the end of the 1922–23 campaign.

Williamson won seven full caps for England, the first against Ireland at Ayresome Park in February 1905. The match ended all-square at 1–1 with Williamson scoring an own goal!

He was ever-present in five seasons - 1903–04, 1906–07, 1908–09, 1909–10 and 1920–21. With the exception of his first two games, Williamson played all his football in the First Division, appearing in 563 League games. All told he appeared in 602 League and Cup games and scored two goals, both from the penalty-spot against Liverpool (Home 2–2 in April 1910), and Bristol City (Home 3–0 in September 1910).

WILSON, ANDY

Andy Wilson played his early football for Cambuslang, a Glasgow junior team before signing for Middlesbrough in February 1914. He made his debut for 'Boro in a 1–0 defeat at West Bromwich Albion but went on to show plenty of promise, scoring five goals in nine games. During the First World War, a shell fragment shattered his arm and he was invalided home. Even though Middlesbrough still held his Football League registration, he was allowed to play for Hearts. Instead of returning to Ayresome Park, he played for breakaway Scottish club, Dunfermline between 1919 and 1921, scoring 104 goals in his two seasons with them. It was whilst playing for Dunfermline that the thoughtful player who kept his forward line together well, won the first of his six full caps for Scotland.

He rejoined Middlesbrough in the summer of 1921 and was the First Division's top scorer the following season with 32 goals in 35 games including hat-tricks in the 3–2 home win over West Bromwich Albion and the 4–1 defeat of Manchester City, also at Ayresome Park. Wilson went on to score 57 goals in 90 games before joining Chelsea for £6,000 in November 1923. At the end of that season both 'Boro and Chelsea were relegated and Wilson had the distinction of being each club's leading scorer!

He repaid Chelsea's faith in him by scoring 62 goals in 235 games before later playing for Queen's Park Rangers and in France. On his return to this country he became manager of Clacton Town before taking charge at Walsall.

WOOD, DARREN

Scarborough-born defender Darren Wood made his Middlesbrough debut in a 2–0 defeat at Southampton in the fifth game of the 1981–82 season when just 17 years old. He appeared in 11 games in that relegation season, scoring his first goal for the club in a 3–0 win over Notts County. In 1982–83 the youngster was one of only two ever-presents as 'Boro finished 16th in Division Two. He repeated the achievement the following season, appearing in 90 consecutive league games in this spell. In September 1984 after scoring six goals in 115 League and Cup games, he left Teeside to join Chelsea, managed by former 'Boro boss, John Neal.

Wood spent four seasons at Stamford Bridge, appearing in 144 league games. Midway through the club's promotion-winning season of 1988–89,

Wood was sold to Sheffield Wednesday but after just 11 appearances for the Owls, he was forced to retire with a back injury.

WORST STARTS

The club's worst-ever start to a season was in 1954–55. It took ten league games to record the first victory of the season, drawing one and losing eight of the opening nine fixtures. The dismal run ended with a 2–1 home win over Lincoln City on 25 September 1954. The club then won five of their next six games and ended the season in 12th place in Division Two.

X

'X'

In football 'x' traditionally stands for a draw. The club record for the number of draws in a season was in 1924–25 when they managed 19 draws out of 42 matches.

XMAS DAY

There was a time when football matches were regularly played on Christmas Day but in recent years, the game's authorities have dropped the fixture from the calendar. The last time Middlesbrough played on Christmas Day was 1957 when they went down 1–0 at Huddersfield Town.

The club's first league game played on Christmas Day 1905 saw them beat Birmingham 1–0 with Alf Common scoring the 'Boro goal.

In 1909, 'Boro went down to what is still their biggest home defeat when they lost 7–3 to Bradford City. On Christmas Day 1926, George Camsell scored all five goals as 'Boro beat Manchester City 5–3 at Maine Road. Two years later they beat Port Vale 5–1 but in 1931 went down to their heaviest Christmas Day defeat when they were beaten 7–1 by Aston Villa.

In the years either side of the Second World War, 'Boro and Leeds United were involved in some high scoring games - 1934 ('Boro 0 Leeds 5), 1937 ('Boro 3 Leeds 5), and 1946 ('Boro 3 Leeds 3). In 1952 Spurs beat Middlesbrough 7–1 to equal Villa's achievement some 21 years previous. The club's last home game on Christmas Day was in 1956 when goals from Clough (2) and Harris helped them beat Doncaster Rovers 3–2.

Y

YORSTON, BENNY

Born at Nigg near Aberdeen, Benny Yorston played junior football for Mugiemoss while working as an office boy for Aberdeen. After a few games in the Dons' third team, he played for Montrose where he won Scottish junior international honours. This prompted Aberdeen to give him another chance and they took him on their 1927 tour of South Africa.

In 1929–30 he set a new club goalscoring record with 38 goals and the following season was capped by Scotland at full international level when he played against Northern Ireland.

In January 1932, Sunderland paid £2,000 for his services but just over two years later after scoring 26 goals in 52 games for the Wearsiders he moved to Middlesbrough. He made his debut for 'Boro at Anfield and though he scored twice, Liverpool won 6–2. He began the 1934–35 season by scoring a hat-trick in the opening match as 'Boro won 4–2 at Leeds United. In the seasons leading up to the war, Yorston created many goalscoring opportunities for Camsell, Birkett and Fenton and though he broke his leg in the match at Blackpool in December 1937 he went on to score 54 goals in 159 games before the Second World War.

During the hostilities he joined the Army Physical Training Corps but ended his playing days shortly afterwards. He later scouted for both Bury and Barnsley before ending his involvement with the game.

YOUNGEST PLAYER

The youngest players to appear in a first-class fixture for Middlesbrough are Sam Lawrie and Stephen Bell who both made their debut at the age of 16 years 323 days. Sam Lawrie made his debut on 3 November 1951 in a 3–0 home defeat by Arsenal whilst Stephen Bell played his first game on 30 January 1982 as 'Boro lost 1–0 at home to Southampton.

YOUTH CUP

Middlesbrough have reached the final of the FA Youth Cup on one occasion and that was in 1989–90. On their way to the final, 'Boro beat Scunthorpe United (Home 2–0 after a 1–1 draw), Notts County (Away 2–0), Ipswich Town (Home 2–0), and West Bromwich Albion (Home 2–0). In the semi-finals, 'Boro won 1–0 at Fratton Park and 3–1 at home to beat Portsmouth 4–1 on aggregate.

In the two-legged final, 'Boro lost 2–1 at home to Spurs and though they drew 1–1 in the second leg at White Hart Lane, they lost 3–2 on aggregate.

Z

ZENITH

Middlesbrough have in recent seasons won the First Division Championship and reached the finals of both the FA and League Cups, yet few fans would argue that the club's first divisional championship winning season of 1926–27 was the finest in the club's history.

Not only did 'Boro score 122 goals, their highest in any campaign and George Camsell establish a new goalscoring record with 59 goals in 37 games but they finished eight points clear of runners-up Portsmouth and third-placed Manchester City.

ZENITH DATA SYSTEMS CUP

The Zenith Data Systems Cup replaced the Simod Cup for the 1989–90 season. Middlesbrough's first match in the competition saw them beat Port Vale 3–1. Further victories over Sheffield Wednesday (Home 4–1), and Newcastle United (Home 1–0), took 'Boro into the two-legged Northern Area Final. Goals from Slaven and Brennan gave Middlesbrough a 2–1 win at Villa Park but after Aston Villa had won 1–0 at Ayresome Park, the tie went into extra-time. Slaven and Kerr scored for 'Boro to give them a 4–2 win on aggregate. Reaching Wembley for the first time in their history, 'Boro lost 1–0 to Chelsea in front of a crowd of 76,369.

In 1990–91 'Boro beat Hull City 3–1 after extra-time but went out of the competition in the next round after losing 2–1 at Manchester City.

In 1991–92, 'Boro found themselves 2–0 down at half-time in their home match against Derby County but second-half goals from Wilkinson (2), Phillips and Slaven gave 'Boro a 4–2 win. The club went out of the competition in the quarter-finals, losing 1–0 to Tranmere Rovers.

ISBN 978-0-260-01122-0
PIBN 10922080

This book is a reproduction of an important historical work. Forgotten Books uses state-of-the-art technology to digitally reconstruct the work, preserving the original format whilst repairing imperfections present in the aged copy. In rare cases, an imperfection in the original, such as a blemish or missing page, may be replicated in our edition. We do, however, repair the vast majority of imperfections successfully; any imperfections that remain are intentionally left to preserve the state of such historical works.

1 MONTH OF FREE READING

at

www.ForgottenBooks.com

By purchasing this book you are eligible for one month membership to ForgottenBooks.com, giving you unlimited access to our entire collection of over 1,000,000 titles via our web site and mobile apps.

To claim your free month visit:

www.forgottenbooks.com/free922080